@-investing

How to Choose and Use a Discount Broker

@-investing

How to Choose and Use a Discount Broker

ROB CARRICK & GUY J. ANDERSON

JOHN WILEY & SONS
Toronto • New York • Chichester • Weinheim • Brisbane • Singapore

John Wiley & Sons Canada Limited
22 Worcester Road
Etobicoke, Ontario
M9W 1L1

Canadian Cataloguing in Publication Data

Carrick, Rob, 1962–
  E-investing : how to choose and use a discount broker

Includes index.
ISBN 0-471-64520-6

1. Discount brokers – Canada. 2. Financial institutions – Canada.
I. Anderson, Guy J., 1969– . II. Title.

HG4621.C37 2000   332.6'2   C00-931003-7

Production Credits
Cover and Text Design: Interrobang Graphic Design Inc.
Printer: Tri-Graphic Printing

Printed and bound in Canada
10 9 8 7 6 5 4 3 2 1

Contents

Introduction

I n the next decade, virtually every home in Canada will have an account at a discount broker. Aggressive stock traders and cautious mutual fund/GIC investors alike will fire up their computers, jump onto the Internet and then log into their discount broker's Web site whenever they want to buy or sell investments. In 1998, there were just 200,000 people trading on-line in Canada. These were the early adopters, many of them lured to on-line trading by the prospect of hitting it big with by playing Nasdaq-listed Internet stocks like Yahoo and Amazon.com. Today, on-line investing has broadened out into the mainstream, but heavy trading days on Nasdaq are still guaranteed to mean busy times for discount brokers. A further widening of the customer base is expected over the next few years. Internet consulting firm Forrester Research of Cambridge, Massachussetts, predicts that by 2003 there will be somewhere in the area of one million Canadians investing electronically. Extend that growth trend out another five years and you have one in six Canadians doing at least some of their investing on their own over the Net.

Conservatively speaking, that is. There are trends at work right now that could easily accelerate the pace of growth. An increasingly savvy investing public is starting to get restive about brokers who dine out on commissions and yet deliver indifferent service and, worse, sub-standard investment returns. Full-service brokers aren't going to disappear—at least the very good ones won't. There will always be a market for smart, honest people to help others manage their money. The endangered brokers are the ones which are mediocre or worse. With on-line investing being so cheap and easy, there's just no reason for anyone to put up with these characters.

Demographics—sorry to bring up this hackneyed phrase, but it applies here—will also accelerate things. The massive baby boom generation is heading toward retirement with the knowledge that people can't leave their financial security to the government any more. Many of these people will realize that the low-cost investing you can do with a discounter is ideal for their Registered Retirement Savings Plans (RRSPs) and Registered Retirement Income Funds (RRIFs). Younger generations will find it hard to imagine investing any way other than on-line. Even those Generation Xers who end up with a financial advisor will maintain discount broker accounts to do some of their own trading.

There's another demographic trend that will work in favor of on-line investing and it has to do with the type of people who are buying stocks these days. Used to be, buying stocks was something that rich people did. Why? Because buying stocks meant having a broker, and that was intimidating, particularly for people who didn't have a lot of money. Many brokers demand large minimum investments, which can eliminate small timers. Today, you can set up an account with most discount brokers with just a few dollars. And since you're working with technology to trade, you don't have to worry about anybody looking down on you. Yes, e-investing is a great equalizer.

Technological change is also widening the appeal of on-line investing. High-speed Internet connections are poised to make an impact in the marketplace, a development that will make on-line investing a more pleasant experience altogether. Traffic-related tie-ups will persist on the Internet, but quotes, graphs and stock-screening tools are going to be a lot more attractive if they're faster to use. Most of the people who don't or won't immediately adopt high-speed service will continue to use 56K modems, which are more than adequate for Internet trading.

The price decline in computers will bring more people to on-line investing as well. Households that couldn't afford computers before now can. These people may not be running six-figure investment portfolios with their on-line brokerage accounts, but they can easily put a little aside occasionally in a mutual fund. Not that having a computer at home is necessary for on-line trading. Fact is, you can do it at work, the library or anywhere else you find a computer.

Amazingly, with all the growth in discount brokerage use so far and the promise of so much more to come, no one has yet produced a manual for on-line investing. You buy a car; you get a manual, which is only proper since a car is a powerful, complex machine. But so is an account at a discount broker, particularly when it's wired for on-line trading over the Internet.

If you already have a discount broker account, this book will show you how to use it more effectively. It will also get you started if you're one of the multitudes who have set up accounts but aren't sure exactly what to do with them. If you've toyed with the idea of using a discount broker, this book may be the spark that gets you going.

It has to be said that discount broker accounts aren't like bank accounts. Not everyone needs or should have one. If you just can't imagine calling your own investing shots and you can't see yourself learning the basics necessary to invest effectively, then you're better off with one of the zillions of bankers, brokers and financial planners out there who would be more than happy to work with you.

But consider this. With a discount broker, you can manage your own money for less than a professional would charge. More than that, it's probable you'll do at least as good a job if you invest sensibly. There's an emotional payoff as well to self-investing. If you've ever heard someone talking about his or her stock market exploits, you know very well that there's an authentic thrill involved in placing your own stock trades.

This is a good place to look at a few misconceptions about discounters. For one thing, investing on-line through a discounter is not the same as day trading. Discount brokers are ideal for investing styles that range from conservative buy-and-hold to speculative short-term investing, but they're next to useless for the split-second timing needed for day trading because of frequent service delays in very active markets.

Also, you don't have to be a high-volume stock trader to use a discount broker. If you want, there's no reason you can't just hold some guaranteed investment certificates (GICs) and mutual funds in your portfolio. Finally, you don't need to be steeped in investing wisdom to use a discount broker, although a least some basic knowledge and a willingness to learn more is required.

In fact, a good way to think of discount brokers is not so much as a means of investing but as a way of realizing the financial goals we set all through our lives. Planning to buy a house? Send your children to university? Just want to increase your net worth? Have any intentions of playing the market for fun and profit? Skillfully used, a discounter broker can help you achieve all these goals.

WHAT EXACTLY IS A DISCOUNT BROKER?

Royal Bank Action Direct (www.actiondirect.com) answers this question succinctly on its Web site's "Frequently Asked Questions" page. A discount brokerage "provides a wide range of services to investors including the execution of orders to buy and sell securities at commission rates often significantly lower than those charged by full-service brokers. Discount brokers do not provide advice or recommendations to clients."

On second thought, this definition is probably a little bleak. Discounters started out being nothing more than a cheap trade, but that's far from the situation today. True, they still don't provide advice or recommendations, but they do give clients access to all kinds of tools and resources they can use to make intelligent investing decisions. Just about any discounter will let you track daily market developments, get quotes and stock price charts for the stocks in your portfolio and, to a limited extent, do research on mutual funds and stocks.

Discounters are also evolving in the way they allow clients to trade and gain access to their accounts. On-line orders now account for 60 to almost 90 per cent of trades, depending on the discounter. But if you're not up for on-line trading, then you should be aware that most discounters also offer the option of trading over the telephone with a live trader or over an automated phone system.

WHAT'S THE HISTORY BEHIND DISCOUNT BROKERS?

From the client's point of view, there were never any good old days in the brokerage business. Twenty years ago, investing in the stock market meant having a broker who would give you investment advice and then have your trades executed. Commissions were high—as much as two or three per cent of the value of the trade. But what could you do? There was no point in shopping around for a better deal because securities regulations prevented firms from competing on the basis of commission costs. Besides, in the old days it was mainly high net worth individuals—rich guys—who played the markets. The very idea of the average person having a brokerage account was awfully close to absurd.

All that changed in April 1983, when the Ontario and Quebec securities commissions opened up the industry to competition on the basis of commissions. It wasn't a bold, visionary move. As is so often the case in Canada's business history, the lead came from the United States. US institutional investors—large pension and mutual funds and insurance companies—started exerting pressure for lower commissions in the years following the Second World War. Fed up with a system that amounted to legalized price-fixing, they launched an unsuccessful challenge of the commission restrictions imposed by the US Securities Exchange Commission. The next step was to start dealing with second-tier brokers, who weren't stock exchange members, a development that caused the elite Wall Street firms to start losing business.

In 1969, the president of the New York Stock Exchange sensed the forces of change at work and proposed to open commissions to competition. That did it. First institutional trades over $500,000 were negotiable, then it was $300,000, and finally, in 1975, individuals and institutions alike were able to negotiate trading commissions. Eventually, discounters moved to commission schedules that generally included low-cost, flat-rate trading. The benefit for investors was that they could receive a discounted commission and also know the commission rate in advance of their trade, rather than negotiating with the broker every time they placed a trade.

In Canada, the US move to deregulate commissions put the brokerage industry under immense pressure to follow suit. But when the Ontario and Quebec securities commissions finally did move on commissions in 1983, it was to a lukewarm reception. It wasn't until the bull market of the late nineties that investors took full advantage of the reduced rates offered by discounters.

Canadians have certainly made up for lost time. The investment industry research firm Investor Economics says there were 2.1 million discount brokerage accounts nationwide by the end of 1999, up 350 per cent from 600,000 five years earlier. Assets held in discount broker accounts surged to $83 billion at the end of 1999, up 488 per cent from $17 billion in 1994.

The first discounter to open for business in Canada was Disnat, a division of the Caisse Desjardins that is now a major player in the Quebec market only. Another early player was Toronto-Dominion Bank's Green Line Investor Services, now the undisputed market share leader in Canada with more than 750,000 clients in Canada. Green Line became TD Waterhouse in 1999 as the bank moved to consolidate the Canadian operation with Waterhouse Securities, the US discounter it bought in 1996 for (Cdn) $726-million. The move created a discount powerhouse that ranks second in the United States, behind Charles Schwab, and ahead of the discount arm of mutual fund giant Fidelity Investments.

Every large Canadian bank now owns a discount broker, but it wasn't always so. TD got into the discount business early on, but the other banks followed only gradually. This was partly because, the banks were acquiring full-service brokers in the latter 1980s and placed a greater priority there. It wasn't until years later that the big banks as a group realized that a discount brokerage was a must-have line of business.

US discounters have had an impact in Canada as well. E*Trade Group Inc. of Menlo Park, California, has licensed its name and technology to a Canadian group, Versus Technologies Inc., while Charles Schwab gained a foothold by taking over discounter

Priority Brokerage Inc. and full-service broker Porthmeor Securities Inc. in early 1999. Since then, there has been a steady flow of rumours of other discounters coming to Canada such as deep discounters Datek Online or Ameritrade. The arrival of U.S. discounters couldn't be better news for investors. Just as the Americans led the way in deregulating commissions, they've also been the most aggressive in both making discount brokers more user-friendly and in slashing commissions.

There are now 12 discounters in Canada, all of them a little different in character, features and cost. In Chapter 2, you'll find a brief overview of each. Throughout the book, you'll notice that discounters are often referred to with the name of their parent bank in front, for example, Royal Bank Action Direct. This is simply to help give brokers an identity in the minds of readers who are unfamiliar with them.

It has to be noted in conclusion that discounters have come in for some angry criticism by clients in recent months because of delays in answering phones and executing trades. What's happening is that more and more people are signing up and trading, and the brokers simply can not handle the volume. It seems that discount brokers have brilliantly dealt with their first big challenge, which was to make people believe that they could invest on their own. The next challenge will be keeping all their new clients satisfied with the service

A word about CT Securities

Toronto-Dominion Bank's purchase of Canada Trust will spell the end for CT Securities as TD Waterhouse converts all CT accounts to the Waterhouse name. Because there was no indication at press time about when this move would be made, we have included full details on CT throughout the book.

1

Discounter Basics

Ask yourself if you're really cut out to handle your own investing through a discounter. We believe almost everyone can do it and do it well. Still, you have to reflect a little on this question. To help you, we've created a questionnaire that delves into your qualifications and level of preparedness for investing on your own. This isn't a scientific process, just a way to offer some guidelines.

But first, a couple of stories. They're aimed at investors who want to skip over this section to get to the stuff about aggressive stock trading. There's nothing wrong with trading hard, in fact your broker will love you for it. Just so you know the risks, though, consider this story based on an actual case.

Our investor expected to pay $3,000 or so for his trade and he ended up being on the hook for $30,000. An investor read in the newspaper one morning that a computer chip company had just received a significant order from a dominant manufacturer of personal computers. This investor decided to place an order for as many of the chip company's shares as she could afford based on the asking price before the market opened of $50. She ended up placing an order for 1,000 shares at the market, which means at the going market rate. She really wanted the stock so she didn't place a limit order, which would have put a cap on what she was willing to pay.

The chip company was listed on Nasdaq, the volatile marketplace that most hot technology stocks call home. As happens so often on this wild market, the company's share price responded to the news overnight and was up $20 to $70 when the market opened. Traders at this investor's discount broker tried to contact her to advise her of the price jump, and that her market order would likely get filled at the higher price, but she wasn't available to take the call because she was in a meeting.

By the time she was able to call back to get confirmation on the trade, she had bought 1,000 shares of the company at $20 more per share than she had anticipated. In the end, she was forced to liquidate the position—sell off her shares—because she didn't have the funds to cover the trade. Unfortunately, the shares had come off their high by this time and the investor took a loss of over $5,000.

You might suggest that this investor should have put in a limit order instead of a market order, but Nasdaq is the kind of fast-moving market where limit orders often don't get filled. You might also say it was a factor of experience. Had she been more seasoned, this investor would have known that shares trading on Nasdaq tend to be quite explosive and that it would be typical for the stock to respond to positive news. It's also possible to argue that she didn't devote the proper time to her investments, that she should have monitored the trade between the time she submitted it and its execution.

Whatever the cause of the loss, the story still boils down to this: Here was an investor who knew enough about the market to place her own trade but didn't have the combination of experience, knowledge and time to make the trade properly.

Now, let's look at that questionnaire.

Questionnaire

The Five Questions:

1. Investment Knowledge
2. Inventory Experience
3. Time Available
4. Ability to Work Solo
5. Technical Savvy

Question 1 - Investment Knowledge

There are really two kinds of knowledge to consider here, the first being pure investing knowledge, things like portfolio allocation basics, the workings of the stock market and the risks posed by various types of securities. The second you might call trading knowledge, which refers to the ins and outs of selecting securities and then buying or selling them advantageously. You don't have to have an encyclopedic understanding of either type of investing knowledge in order to use a discount broker, but you do need to know the basics and where to go to get more detailed information. It's also important to be aware that if you describe yourself as having a complete lack of knowledge about investing, your broker could conceivably reject your account application.

Here's a quick way to assess your level of investment knowledge. If you're a knowledgeable or sophisticated investor you will have a detailed working knowledge of how the financial markets work and how to effectively manage your own portfolio. Someone with average or a low level of knowledge would have a limited understanding of the markets. Ultimately, it's not a matter of having knowledge of every arcane matter of investing but of knowing the principles and where to find the answers.

My investment knowledge is:

Sophisticated	5 points
Moderately strong	4
Average	3
Low	2
Non-existent	1

My Point Score: _____

Question 2 - Investing Experience

First, consider what type of investing you plan to do with a discounter. Then think about your relevant experience. If you intend to buy stocks and your experience is limited to GICs and mutual funds, you may be getting in over your head. On the other hand, you may be a novice who has done a lot of reading on investing matters and is looking at setting up a discount broker account to put into practice what you've learned. In fact, using a discount broker is an ideal way to gain experience because you exercise complete control over your investing.

It's worth noting that when discounters themselves mention investing experience, they generally mean familiarity with stock trading. There's a good reason for this—clients at most brokers have 50 to 70 per cent of their assets in stocks, with the remainder divided up between mutual funds, options and bonds.

I would describe myself as:

A seasoned stock trader	5 points
An occasional but experienced stock trader	4
An infrequent or novice trader who has read a lot on the subject	3
A mutual funds-only type	2
Experienced only with GICs and CSBs (Canada Savings Bonds)	1

My Point Score: _____

Question 3 - Time Available

The more aggressive you plan to be in your investing, the more time you'll need to spend on your portfolio. Hour-by-hour monitoring of a trade through your computer may be necessary if you're trading volatile high-tech stocks. Even if you're a buy-and-hold investor, you'll still need to spend time periodically reviewing things. An investor with little or no time to spend might sensibly choose a managed account at a full-service broker or a mutual fund.

**The amount of time I have to devote
to my investments is:**

An hour or two a night	5 points
An hour or two a week	4
An hour or two a month	3
A few hours every six months	2
A few hours or less a year	1

My Point Score: _____

Question 4 - Ability to Work Solo

You can ask the staff at a discount broker about technical things like services and fees, but you won't get any advice on investing options or strategies. Can you live with this, or would you feel more comfortable having someone to guide you?

My ideal way of investing would be to:

Research everything myself	5 points
Research myself plus look at research by professionals	4
Sometimes discuss my investments with a professional	3
Have an adviser recommend investments	2
Stick to GICs and funds sold by my bank	1

My Point Score: _____

Question 5 - Technical Savvy

You can trade through a discounter and never touch a computer, but that's like buying a sports car and never taking it on the highway. On-line trading is cheaper, plus you can get access to market news, quotes, charts and research tools. To go on-line, though, you need to be at ease with computers.

I'm perfectly comfortable:

Investing and researching over the Internet without human contact	5 points
Using the Internet mostly but sometimes consulting live humans	4
Using the Internet a little but mostly using the phone	3
Talking over the telephone with a live person only	2
Only when I have face-to-face contact when investing	1

My Point Score: _____

How to Read Your Score

A perfect 25:
You're a natural for a discounter. If you haven't already got an account, what are you waiting for?

20 to 24:
Going with a discounter would make a lot of sense for you.

15 to 19:
If you feel comfortable making your own investing calls, then a discounter may be the right way to go.

10 to 14:
You may not be ready for a discounter. Read this book and re-evaluate yourself.

0 to 9:
A discounter isn't right for you at this time.

One last consideration in making the decision about whether to use a discounter is portfolio size. Size matters, but not because the wealthy deserve better treatment than those with smaller portfolios. Rather, it's because larger portfolios have more complex needs in areas such as estate preservation, tax minimization and asset allocation than others. If you have a portfolio in the $100,000-plus range, you have to ask yourself if you can do better managing your money than professionals with resources like accountants and lawyers.

Who is the typical discount brokerage client? As we saw in the introduction, discounters are appropriate for people from all walks of life. Here are three investor profiles that help illustrate this.

DISCOUNT BROKER CLIENT PROFILE 1: Susan is a 57-year- old university-educated middle manager who has been dealing with a full-service broker for years. She has a sizable portfolio and she regularly researches her own investments before making a buy or sell decision. She rarely hears from her broker, usually only at her annual review. She has decided to slowly move her investments to a discounter, reasoning that the attention she's received from her advisor doesn't warrant the minimum $100 commission per trade she pays since she does her own research anyway.

DISCOUNT BROKER CLIENT PROFILE 2: George is a 27-year-old MBA graduate who realizes the value of qualitative and quantitative analysis. He's technically savvy and spends much of his time on-line researching stocks and reading the most recent news releases. He's never used a full-service broker since he can't justify paying five times the commission he would through his on-line broker. Since he's on-line much of the day he likes the freedom of trading with his discount brokerage firm through the Internet and regularly reviews his portfolio. His bank has an associated full-service broker, but it doesn't yet permit on-line trading so it's not even an option.

DISCOUNT BROKER CLIENT PROFILE 3: Allison and Ken are a young couple who are investing neophytes. They don't have much experience in the market, in fact they have only invested in

mutual funds at their bank. They have been influenced by the
hype behind the market performance of the past few years,
and discount broker advertising, and have recently opened
their account to get their feet wet. Since they are new
investors they cannot justify paying $85 with their bank's
associated broker, given that their investments themselves
would generally be less than $1,000.

So far, we've looked at ways of deciding whether a discount
broker is right for you based on your level of investing knowledge, experience and so forth. Now, let's fill in some details on
how discount brokers actually work.

How Do I Do Business with a Discount Broker?

The quick answer here is: just about any way you want, even
face-to-face. Discounters now receive at least two-thirds of their
buy and sell orders over the Internet. The remaining trades are
done over the telephone with a live agent, over an automated
phone service or through new telephone voice-recognition technology that allows you to speak your order to a computer. Here's
how each of the access channels works:

FACE-TO-FACE CONTACT

The opportunity for a prospective client to walk into an office
and discuss opening an account is a great confidence-builder.
The largest US discounter, Charles Schwab, does about 70 per
cent of new account sign-ups through its extensive branch network, even though 80 per cent of its trades are done on-line.

No Canadian discount brokers have such a large branch network, although TD Waterhouse, the largest Canadian discounter,
comes close on a proportional basis. Most other discounters
maintain at least a few walk-in offices in major centres across the
country where you can pose questions to knowledgeable account
representatives, browse for brochures and sometimes even pick
up a phone or access a computer to place a trade. In some cases,
you can also walk into a city's major bank branches and speak
with a representative of the related discount broker.

Walk-in Investor Centre and Office Locations
(check your broker's Web site for the most up-to-date information)

Bank of Montreal InvestorLine
(6 locations)
First Canadian Place
100 King St. W., 20th Floor
Toronto, ON M5X 1A1
(416) 867-4000

Commerce Gate
505, Highway 7
Thornhill, ON L3T 7T6
(416) 867-4000, press 2

First Canadian Centre
350 - 7th Avenue SW, 7th Floor
Calgary, AB T2P 3N9
(403) 262-7000

2609 Granville Street, Suite 310
Vancouver, BC V6H 3H2
(604) 665-7000

2015 Peel Street, 2nd Floor
Montreal, QC H3A 1T8
(514) 877-2100

5151 George St., 1st Floor
Halifax, NS B3J 2M3
(902) 421-3606

Bank of Montreal Investore
1 First Canadian Place
100 King Street West, Concourse Level
Toronto, ON M5X 1A1
(416) 643-1778

LimeRidge Mall
999 Upper Wentworth
Hamilton, ON L9A 4X5
(905) 574-7834

Masonville Place Mall
1680 Richmond Street North
London, ON N6G 3Y9
(519) 645-6634

5th Avenue Place
#108, 425-1st Street SW
Calgary, AB T2P 3L8
(403) 216-3740

Richmond Shopping Centre
6551 Number 3 Road
Richmond, BC V6Y 2B6
(604) 668-1233

Charles Schwab Canada
207 Queen's Quay West, Suite 800
P.O. Box 134
Toronto, ON M5J 1A7
(416) 359-1900
1-888-597-9999

The Exchange Tower
130 King St. W.
P.O. Box 268 / Main Floor
Toronto, ON M5X 1C9

Market Village
4372 Steeles Avenue East
Unit G13, Box 48
Markham, ON L3R 9V6

1411 Peel Street,
Suite 200 Mezzanine Level
Montreal, QC H3A 1S5

466 Howe Street/ Main Floor
Vancouver, BC V6C 2X1

Coming in 2000:
Richmond, B.C.
Ottawa
Halifax
Calgary

CIBC Investor's Edge
No locations. Clients and
prospective clients can discuss
the Investor's Edge service with
staff at more than 1,300 CIBC
branches across Canada.

CT Securities
161 Bay St., Concourse Level
Toronto, ON

1501 McGill College Ave.
Montreal, QC

Disnat
2020 University, 9th Floor
Montreal, QC H3A 2A5
(514) 842-2685
1-800-268-8471

2600, boul. Laurier
9th floor, Suite 2940
Sainte-Foy, QC
G1V 4M9
(418) 650-5898
1-800-463-1887

E*Trade Canada
60 Yonge St., 12th Floor
Toronto, ON M5E 1H5

181 Bay St.
Toronto, ON M5J 2T3

HSBC InvestDirect
70 York Street, 16th Floor
Toronto, ON M5J 1S9

3640 Victoria Park Avenue
Willowdale, ON M2H 3B2

30 Metcalfe Street
Ottawa, ON K1P 5L4

Good Fortune Plaza
212,111 - 3rd Avenue, SE
Calgary, AB T2G 0B7

777 - 8th Avenue, SW
Calgary, AB T2P 3R5

885 West Georgia, Main Floor
Vancouver, BC V6C 3G1

Wayfoong House, Main Floor
608 Main Street
Vancouver, BC V6C 3K4

1000-888 Dunsmuir Street
Vancouver, BC V6A 2V8

1010-4380 #3 Road
Richmond, BC V6X 3V7

Fortuna House
6168 #3 Road
Richmond, BC V6X 2B3

National Bank Discount Brokerage
1100 University St., 7th floor
Montreal, QC H3B 2G7

TD Waterhouse
Home Oil Tower
324-8th Avenue SW, Suite 1200
Calgary, AB T2P 2Z2
(403) 292-2875
1-800-472-9717

2503 Toronto Dominion Tower
Edmonton Centre
Edmonton, AB T5J 2Z1
(403) 448-8088
1-800-350-4832

1791 Barrington Street, Suite 510
Halifax, NS B3J 2T3
(902) 423-1171
1-800-565-0769

Stelco Tower
100 King Street West, Suite 310
Hamilton, ON L8P 1A2
(905) 521-1073
1-800-263-8560

410 Bernard Avenue, Suite 200
Kelowna, BC V1Y 7N3
(250) 717-8100
1-800-668-8166

115 Clarence Street
Kingston, ON K7L 5N6
(613) 549-1609
1-800-387-1407

381 King Street, 2nd Floor
Kitchener, ON N2G 1B8
(519) 571-6080
1-800-661-6350

3080 Boul le Carrefour, Suite 150
Laval, QC H7T 2R5
(514) 973-3141
1-800-451-1647

520 - 4th Ave. S, Unit J
Lethbridge, AB T1J 2C9
(403) 317-4800
1-888-561-4966 (Alberta only)

Talbot Centre
148 Fullarton Street, Suite 1103
London, ON N6A 5P3
(519) 660-4225
1-800-265-4447

4300 Steeles Ave. East, Unit B99
Markham, ON L3R 0Y5
(905) 479-5020;
1-888-463-5333

860 Main Street
Moncton, NB, E1C 8M1
(506) 853-4320

500 St. Jacques Street, 6th Floor
Montreal, QC H2Y 1S1
(514) 289-8439
1-800-363-1171

300 - 6581 Aulds Road
Nanaimo, BC V9T 6J6
(250) 390-5940; 1-888-255-5522

Towne Square
210 Lakeshore Road East
Oakville, ON L6J 1H8
(905) 337-3779
1-800-279-4401

Minto Place
427 Laurier Avenue West,
2nd Floor
Ottawa, ON K1R 7Z1
(613) 783-6322
1-800-267-8844

2nd Floor, 400 Victoria Street
Prince George, BC V2L 2G7
(250) 614-2900
1-888-561-4977

2600 Laurier Blvd, Bureau 20
Ste-Foy, QC G1V 4T3
(418) 654-0700
1-800-363-1531

4902 Gaetz Avenue, Suite 201
Red Deer, AB T4N 4A8
(403) 340-7480
1-888-221-2271

Toronto-Dominion Tower
1904 Hamilton St., Suite 940
Regina, SK S4P 3N5
(306) 525-3370
 1-800-667-9951

London Plaza
100-5951 No. 3 Road
Richmond, BC V6X 2E3
(604) 654-8880
1-888-622-8222

Park Place Corporate Centre
15 Wertheim Court, Suite 107
Richmond Hill, ON L4B 3H7
(905) 771-8580
1-800-668-2139

2 King Street, 2nd Floor
Saint John, NB E2L 4E3
(506) 635-4176
1-800-561-2279

TD Place
140 Water Street, Suite 1002
St. John's, NF A1C 6H6
(709) 758-5083
1-800-357-5434

410-22nd Street East, Suite 840
Saskatoon, SK S7K 5T6
(306) 975-739
1-800-667-6856

43 Elm Street, Suite 210
Commerce Court
Sudbury, ON P3C 1S4
(705) 670-8785
1-800-463-9282

1039 Memorial Ave.
Thunder Bay, ON P7B 4A4
(807) 626-1650

Toronto-Dominion Centre
Concourse Level One
55 King Street West
Toronto, ON M5K 1A2
(416) 982-7981
1-800-268-8209

20 York Mills Road, Suite 420
North York, ON M2P 2C2
(416) 944-4274
1-800-268-8270

590 Howe Street,
Pacific Centre Mall
Vancouver, BC V7Y 1E8
(604) 654-3783
1-800-663-0480

TD Bank, 418 Main St.
Vancouver, BC V6A 2T4
(604) 654-6988

1760 Marine Drive
West Vancouver, BC V7V 1J6
(604) 981-4500

1070 Douglas Street, Suite 460
Victoria, BC V8W 2C4
(250) 356-4054
1-800-661-2088

TD Bank, 404 Dundas St. W.
Whitby, ON L1N 2M7
(905) 668-1004

15120 North Bluff Road
White Rock, BC V4B 2E5
(604) 541-2050
1-888-877-5777

586 Ouellette Avenue, Suite 300
Windsor, ON N9A 1B8
(519) 252-7703
1-800-265-0846

201 Portage Avenue, Suite 1617
Winnipeg, MB R3C 3E7
(204) 988-2641
1-800-665-8705

Sun Life Securities
225 King Street West, 5th Floor
Toronto, ON M5V 3C5

1155 Metcalfe Street, Suite 646
Montreal, QC H3B 2V9

Scotia Discount Brokerage
1709 Hollis St., 3rd floor
Halifax, NS B3J 1W1
(902)-420-3727
1-800-665-5559

1002 Sherbrooke St. W., Suite 270
Montreal, QC H3A 3L6
(514) 499-5877
1-800-361-660

1 Richmond St. W., 7th floor
Toronto, ON M5H 3W4
(416) 866-2014

40 King St. W., 5th floor,
Toronto, ON M5H 1H1
(416) 866-2006
1-800-263-3430

8th Aveneue SW, 5th floor
Calgary, AB T2P 3S8
(403) 221-6966
1-800-661-1955

602 Hastings St., 5th floor
Vancouver, BC V6B 1P3
(604) 668-2041
1-800-561-3646

Royal Bank Action Direct
5161 George Street, 7th Floor
Halifax, NS
(902) 421-7954

1 Place Ville Marie
West Wing, 2nd Floor
Montreal, QC
(514) 874-6895

Place Sainte-Foy,
2450-2 Boul Laurier
Sainte-Foy, QC
(418) 654-2477

50 St. Charles Blvd.
Beaconsfield, QC
(514) 630-5253

260 East Beaver Creek Rd,   220 Portage Avenue, Main Floor
Suite 404   Winnipeg, MB
Richmond Hill, ON   (204) 988-5356
(905) 764-5069

                                   335 - 8th Avenue SW, 8th Floor
Royal Bank Plaza   Calgary, AB
200 Bay Street   (403) 299-5190
Toronto, ON
(416) 974-7493   16909 - 103A Avenue
                                   Edmonton, AB
Yonge & Orchardview   (780) 448-6742
2346 Yonge St.
Toronto, ON   1055 West Georgia Street,
(416) 974-2737   Suite 1220
                                   Vancouver, BC
                                   (604) 668-4439

BY PHONE

In the old days, investors had to contact their brokers by phone to inquire about their account or to place trades. This doesn't sound like a hardship, but it was in some cases. If you were out of town, for instance, you'd have to pay the long-distance bill to talk to your broker. You might have tried calling collect, but the broker would likely have taken the call only if you were a major client.

Today, discount clients can dial up a call centre through a toll-free 1-800 number, usually anywhere in North America. Since securities regulations require that brokers and traders be licensed in the province in which they trade, most discounters have set up call centres in different regions of the country. Most have a location in Atlantic Canada (Halifax), Quebec (Montreal), Ontario (Toronto), the Prairies (Calgary) and British Columbia (Vancouver). Each region will have its own toll-free number, while major cities will have a local number to call. The new client kit you receive when you set up an account will help you find the appropriate number to call. This isn't a mere detail—if you live in Alberta and call the Ontario call centre, the people serving you won't be able to handle your trade.

If you're travelling, the rule is that a trade must be placed at the office nearest to where you live. If you're visiting Calgary from the Atlantic region and your discounter has an office in Calgary, any trades you make would still have to be placed with the Halifax office.

Discount broker call centres are designed to handle large volumes of calls. State-of-the-art switching equipment ranks the calls according to the order in which they are received, regardless of whether the call was received through the 1-800 number or the local one. Calling a discounter's 1-800 number is like dialing any other big institution. Generally, you'll be connected to an interactive voice response system (IVR), which is a fancy term for a taped message that offers you a menu of choices that includes trading, quotes and account inquiries. If you're calling to place a trade, you'll be connected to a broker (also called a trader, an investment representative or, less flatteringly, an order-taker) whose job it is to take down the details of your order and then enter it into the firm's execution system for routing to the TSE's computerized trading network. The broker's investing qualifications will generally be at least the Canadian Securities Course (CSC), which is the bare minimum certification for working in the financial industry, as well as an ethics course called the Conducts and Practices Handbook (CPH). Many others will have also completed the Canadian Options Course or equivalent.

Broker/traders should be able to give you detailed information about the products their firms can sell you, but don't bother asking for anything in the way of advice or recommendations. Giving such information is strictly against the rules. And while it's entirely reasonable to expect politeness and a helpful attitude from a broker, the reality is that you'll likely be connected to someone who is overworked and just wants to get on to the next call in the queue. Have a little sympathy—the average order-taker may handle 120 to 150 calls per day.

Figure 1: Discounter Hours of Operation for Live Agent Telephone Service

Bank of Montreal InvestorLine	24/7
Charles Schwab	7 to 7 Monday to Friday
CIBC Investor's Edge	24/7
CT Securities	24/7
Disnat	8 to 6 Monday to Friday ; 10 to 2 Saturday
E*Trade Canada	8 a.m. to 8 p.m., Monday to Friday
HSBC InvestDirect	6:00 a.m. to 3:30 a.m. Monday to Thursday; 6 a.m. to 8 p.m. Fridays; 6 p.m. to 3:30 Sunday
National Bank Discount Brokerage	8 to 9 Monday to Friday
Royal Bank Action Direct	8 a.m. to 6:30 p.m. (8 a.m. to 11 p.m. in Ontario)
Scotia Discount Brokerage	8 a.m. to 8 p.m. Monday to Friday
Sun Life Securities	8 a.m. to 8 p.m., Monday to Friday
TD Waterhouse	24/7

*Some brokers may have expanded their hours. Check for the latest information.

Many discounters offer their telephone clients the option of dealing with live humans or an automated phone system. If you've ever tried to call someone at a big company and had to spell their name on the phone keypad to get their extension, then you have a pretty good idea of how the technology for the automated phone trading and quote system works. Following taped instructions, you press various combinations of numbers and letters to indicate the amount of stocks or mutual funds you want to buy or sell, and so forth. You then use the letters on the keypad to spell out the symbols of the securities you want to trade or hear quotes on.

VIA THE INTERNET: For many people, discount brokers and on-line trading are synonymous. In fact, the allure of Internet trading is one of the main reasons for the phenomenal growth of discount brokers in the past couple of years. What's so great about Internet trading? It's cheap, it's easy, it's fast in most—but definitely not all—circumstances and it can be done on any reasonably powerful computer equipped with a modem and a hook-up to an Internet service provider. All you have to do to start trading is head to your broker's site on the World Wide Web (each Web site is like a mini-neighborhood in the Internet cyber-universe), then type in your user name and password. (See Chapter Four for more detail on how to get set up for Internet trading.)

Internet trading is great for clients but there are quite a few benefits for brokers themselves as well. Imagine the savings discounters realize over their full-service counterparts by maintaining call centres and a Web site rather than a costly network of branches with expensive overhead. One study done by a Internet research firm found that trades placed through a live agent cost US$13 on average, while those placed electronically cost roughly $1. The Web site can also supply reams of information that customers would otherwise have to get by telephone, probably with a wait on hold. Virtually all Web sites provide stock and mutual fund quotes, some in real time and others delayed by 15 to 20 minutes. Most also allow clients to do stock and mutual fund research, set up a phantom portfolio of stocks and get price updates at any time. One of the best things about the Web is that it lets customers check their account holdings at any time. Accounts are generally updated each evening, after the trading day is over.

Let's look more closely at the reasons why buying mutual funds, stocks and options is best done on the Internet (on-line bond trading is starting to become available as well). Certainly, it's the cheapest way to go. At TD Waterhouse, for example, a trade that cost $43 in commission over the telephone with a live representative would be reduced to $29 on the Internet. And then there's speed. Yes, Web trading can bog down so badly you'll sometimes just have to give up and try again later. Generally, though, it takes far less time to call up your broker's Web site order screen than it does to dial the

1-800 number, press all the necessary keys and wait for someone to take your call. Bear in mind as well that clients may have to wait to talk to a trader on a busy day. In early 2000, waits of one hour or more were not uncommon.

OTHER CHANNELS: On-line and phone trading account for the vast majority of trades, but there are a few new channels as well. The latest innovation in the discounter's repertoire is the voice-recognition phone service. TD Waterhouse introduced this service in the fall of 1999 for quotes for Canadian and US stocks and options and Canadian mutual funds and then expanded it for trading. The system works like the automated phone trading system in that you're given prompts about how to proceed, but instead of pressing buttons you use simple one- or two-word spoken commands. Another new development is trading through cellular phones equipped with Web browsers. Just try and find features like this at a full-service broker.

Figure 2: Getting a Quote for Nortel Networks
on TD Waterhouse's TalkBroker System

Step One:	Dial the 1-800 number
Step Two:	The prompt will say, "Please speak or key in your account number."
Step Three:	The prompt will say, "Please speak or key in your password." This refers to your four-digit trading password.
Step Four:	The prompt will say, "Would you like quotes, market monitor, account inquiry, order entry or personal profile?" Say, "Quotes."
Step Five:	The prompt will say, "Would you like Canadian equities, US equities, options or Canadian mutual funds?" Say, "Canadian equities."
Step Six:	The prompt will say, "Please say a Canadian company or index." Say, "Nortel Networks."

A sample of what you might hear in the end: "Nortel Networks. Last price, $173.90 up $20.90. Uptick. (Meaning that the most recent trade was higher than the previous one.) Next company or main menu."

How Much Can I Save With A Discounter?

There are lots of good reasons to invest with a discounter, but ultimately it all comes down to saving money. If you want to buy a full range of Canadian and foreign stocks and mutual funds, you can do it cheaper through a discounter than you can through a full-service broker. If you look at the commissions charged by full-service brokers, you'll see they haven't come all that far from the old days when investment dealers were required to abide by a fee schedule dictating that trades of certain values were to be charged certain commissions.

The rates, set by provincial securities commissions and standard across Canada, were about 3 per cent for shares valued at less than five dollars and two per cent and five cents a share for stocks between $5 and $15. For stocks worth more than $15 the minimum commission was one per cent and 20 cents per share.

Faced with the price challenge posed by discounters, full-service brokers did lower their commissions to the extent that they now have minimum commissions of $85 to $100 typically. They're still more expensive, though—way more expensive. How much is tough to pin down exactly, but several discounters advertise on their Web sites that they can save you up to about 88 per cent in brokerage fees, a statement based on periodic polling of full-service brokers. When you look at the fine print, however, some brokers say the numbers are based on survey results that date back to anywhere from 1996 to 1999. It's hard to believe that the margin of savings discounters offer over full-service brokers hasn't changed at all over a span of four years.

To get the latest perspective on commissions we turned to Bank of Montreal InvestorLine, one of the discounters that prominently plays up the 88-per-cent figure. InvestorLine reported back that it could actually save a little more than 88 per cent in extreme cases. The discounter said its research shows that one unnamed Canadian full-service broker has posted commission rates that would put a fee of $765.40 on a purchase of 1,000 shares of an $85 stock. InvestorLine would charge $25 for the same trade if it were a market order and $29 if it were a limit order, a savings of 96 per cent or so on the market order. We'll go into more detail on market and limit orders in Chapter 6, but basically, a market order says you're willing to accept or pay the going price for a stock, while a limit order specifies exactly what price you will pay, or would like to receive.

Cheaper transactions bring smaller but still significant savings. InvestorLine's research shows the same broker would charge $83.43 to buy you 100 shares of a $25 stock, a savings of about 70 per cent on a market order. Bear in mind, these are the full-service broker's posted rates. Most likely, you'd get a better deal if you were a client who does a lot of trading, has a sizable portfolio or is just a good negotiator. Full-service brokers will undoubtedly have to get more competitive with their commissions, but don't expect them to get into low-cost trading any time soon. With their high-priced analysts and mahogany-panelled offices, the full-service crowd simply has to charge more. Discounters, by comparison, exist only to enter a client's trade quickly and error-free, for a low but still profitable commission.

Figure 3: InvestorLine's Commissions Versus a Full-Service Broker*

Size of Trade	Full Service	InvestorLine
100 shares @ $85	$130	$25/$29
100 shares @ $25	$83	$25/$29
100 shares @ $10	$80	$25/$29
1000 shares @ $85	$765	$25/$29
1000 shares @ $25	$510	$25/$29
1000 shares @ $10	$294	$25/$29

*Representative commission charges based on posted rates quoted from a major Canadian full-service broker. You may be able to negotiate lower rates.
(Source: InvestorLine)

What Other Differences Are there Between Discounters and Full-Service Brokers?

Let's look at the term full-service broker. What it means is that the client has investment advisers who give you personalized service, including an investment plan tailored to your age, investing objectives and risk tolerance; recommendations on securities to buy; research by professional analysts on stocks and mutual funds and access to initial public offerings. If you have a question or want some advice quickly, you can call your broker directly during business hours. Of course, you may just reach your broker's voice mail, or assistant.

Now let's look in greater detail how discounters and full-service brokers compare:

Advice

Discount broker representatives are not permitted under securities regulations to offer advice, even if asked by a customer. In this respect, discount brokerage reps are more like order-takers than traditional brokers. Similar to the sweat shops of an earlier era, these people are measured more by the number of calls they take and trades they place than by the service or information they can provide the client. Discount reps are for the most part on salary, often with an incentive bonus based on the financial performance of the parent company, which is usually a bank. Investment advisers, on the other hand, are commissioned sales people who only make money when clients place trades. Naturally, this leads to the question of who really benefits from a trade, the client or broker.

One exception to the advice-free nature of discounters is Charles Schwab Canada, which offers clients the option of working with a (salaried) advisor. If you use the advice option at Schwab, you pay more in commissions.

Responsibilities to the Client

The discounter's main responsibility is to have client trades executed at the best possible price. An investment adviser's key responsibility is to follow the Know Your Client rule, which requires that securities be recommended only if they are suitable to a client's risk tolerance and investing objectives. Until recently, discounters were bound by the KYC rule in that they had to perform a suitability check on each client trade. This has changed in recognition of the fact that discounters do not provide advice or recommendations.

Training

Discount staff and full-service investment advisers have to meet the same minimum industry standards—the Canadian Securities Course (CSC) and the ethics course, Conducts and Practice Handbook (CPH). Discounters may require their staff to pass an internal exam before being granted permission to place trades. Full-service brokers are required to pass a professional financial planning course within a set period after being licensed. All courses are run by the Canadian Securities Institute, which is an arm of the Investment Dealers Association of Canada.

Research

Larger full-service brokerages have a specialized research department, something that discounters do not have. If you're a discount client who wants research reports written by analysts, you can either buy third-party material or in some cases receive reports from analysts working elsewhere in the corporate family that owns your discount broker. As an example, TD Waterhouse sells reports by TD Securities analysts (unless you have a premium account in which case the reports are free).

Without a doubt, research by a seasoned analyst is a valuable investing tool. Still, there are reasons to be wary of this resource. Ideally, a full-service dealer would employ dozens of analysts who spend their days dissecting the companies they follow and then distilling their research into well-reasoned recommendations to buy, hold or sell stocks. The reality is somewhat different. Often, analysts follow the same companies their firms are advising in one way or another. There are precious few analysts who would slam the stock of a company that is paying the firm for its expertise. The result is that analysts may stick with buy recommendations on stocks they know to be a disaster area. In fact, sell orders are a rarity among analysts at the major brokers. There have been lots of very shrewd calls by analysts that have made investors money over the years, but there have been many money-losers as well. Just think of Eaton's, Bre-X, Loewen Group, Philip Services and so on.

Communication

Dealing with a discount broker is an anonymous experience. If you trade by phone, you may never speak to the same person twice. On the other hand, you can trade or look at your account at any time on the Internet. If you telephone, you'll have a 1-800 number to use from anywhere in North America and a chance of speaking to someone reasonably quickly provided that you're not calling at peak trading hours. There's no personalized service here, but then again there's no voice mail to put up with, either.

Full-service brokers are starting to make use of the Internet, but they're still miles behind discounters. The typical full-service broker site might offer some of its buy and sell recommendations and economic reports to clients, as well as limited market updates and quotes. Some may allow clients to look up their accounts on-line. The discount broker is generally out there on its Web site, warts and all. You'll find everything from commission schedules to descriptions of the products sold, market news and tools for researching stocks and funds. More importantly, you can trade through a discount broker Web site.

Account Start-Up

Potential discount broker clients sometimes think the sign-up process is a mere formality, but that's far from true. Account application forms are detailed and have to be completed without omissions. The general guideline is that it takes 24 to 48 hours before an account number is assigned and the client is able to place a trade. Leave out any information and it can take substantially longer to be able to start trading. At a full-service broker, your investment adviser or an assistant will help you fill out the application forms and prevent any omissions or errors. Once the form is completed, you should be able to trade (see Chapter Three for more details on how to set up an account).

Increasingly, investors have sized up the difference between full-service and discount brokers and gone the discount route. Investor Economics says assets in full-service broker accounts grew by two-and-a-half times between 1994 and September 1999, to $335-billion from $137 billion. Discount brokerage assets exploded fourfold over that period, rising to $70-billion from $17 billion. Full-service brokers in Canada don't market themselves directly against discounters, probably because the banks that control them also own discount brokers as well. So let's turn to a US outfit, St. Louis-based Edward Jones, for some insight on how a full-service dealer differentiates itself from a discounter.

Edward Jones issued a newsletter to clients late last year with an article titled: "When a Discount is Not a Bargain: How Much Do You Really Save with a Discounter?" The article, written by chief market strategist Alan Skrainka, makes the claim that while people may feel smarter about financial matters, it's questionable whether they really are. It then argues that while you'll save on commissions with a discounter, you may also make less from your investments.

Figure 4: Edward Jones suggests taking this quiz to see if you need the help of an investing professional.

1. When is it time to sell a stock or a mutual fund?

2. How much of your portfolio should be in stocks, bonds or cash at this stage of your life?

3. How much of your portfolio should be invested in technology stocks, health care or financial services?

4. When is it appropriate to buy more of an investment that has fallen in value?

5. How much can you reasonably expect to earn from your investments?

(Reprinted with permission from Edward Jones)

Having trouble with any of these questions? If so, it's a sign you need to do some research and not necessarily a warning that you shouldn't use a discounter. You can answer all these questions by looking at some of the Web sites that are listed at the end of this chapter.

What Are the Risks of Using a Discount Broker?

No matter what you do in the investing realm, there are risks. Let's take a look at some of the main risks that confront the discount broker client.

Investor Error

We'll look more at this in Chapter Six, but there are a variety of costly errors that investors can make in buying securities through a discounter. A mistake as plain as using a market order instead of a limit order can cost you big time as we saw at the beginning of the chapter. Of course, there are times when you must place a market order if you want your trade executed. If you do, you could make a mistake in the instructions you give your broker and end up paying more for your order than you expected.

Market Risk

Anyone who invests faces this risk, yet it deserves special mention here because you're flying solo when you use a discounter and have no one to remind you that your portfolio may be too heavily weighted to stocks, for example. If you're speculating as opposed to investing for the long term, the risk of taking a loss is even higher.

There are many ways to limit market risk, but it cannot be avoided completely. One way would be to diversify your portfolio, either by purchasing a variety of stocks from different economic sectors or by investing in mutual funds or actual stock indexes through securities such as S&P/TSE 60 participation units—i60s.

In addition to market risk, there is non-market risk, or the danger posed by individual securities. Even the blandest utility stock out there offers certain risks, although they're hardly worth commenting on when compared to Internet stocks and junior mining companies.

Brokerage Collapse

It's highly unlikely, but a broker (whether full-service or discount) could go broke and thereby put your assets at risk. If this happened and your broker was a member of the Canadian Investor Protection Fund (CIPF), then all or most of your assets would be protected. CIPF was established in 1969 and protects investors in case of insolvency. Funded by its members, the fund covers the investor for up to $1 million in losses related to cash or securities. These are not losses from the trading of securities, but rather from the insolvency of the firm itself. Ask your discounter if it's a CIPF member, or check directly with CIPF itself at at **www.cipf.ca** or by calling (416) 866-8366, or writing: P.O. Box 192, 200 Bay St., Toronto, ON, M5J 2J4.

Figure 5: The Seven Myths About Discount Brokers

Myth #1 – Discount brokers are only for investment experts. You must know what investments you want to purchase when you call a discount broker. You should research any potential investments. Information about potential investments is widely available in newspapers, newsletters, libraries, magazines and on the Internet.

Myth #2 – Dealing with a discount broker is complicated. Most discount brokers offer a complete "welcome kit" that contains detailed information on how to get started. If you deal with one of the bank-owned firms, you can usually sign up at your local bank branch. And if you require additional help placing an order, a discount broker can help you over the telephone.

Myth #3 – Discount brokers only trade stocks. Discount brokers offer a full range of investments. You can purchase everything from GICs from a variety of issuers, a choice of hundreds of the most popular mutual funds, bonds, stocks and much more.

Myth #4 – Discount brokers are only for the rich. Anyone wanting access to a wider range of investments and the benefit of paying lower commission fees uses discount brokers. Discount brokerage clients have accounts of varying sizes and with a diversified range of investments.

Myth #5 – Discount brokers deal only with risky investments. You can use a discount broker to buy something as safe and conservative as Canada Savings Bonds or Guaranteed Investment Certificates. Or your investment can be as complex as you need to match your investment experience. The choice is up to you.

Myth #6 – Discount brokers are only for active traders. Most discount brokers are set up to handle just about any investor. You do not need to buy and sell on a regular basis to benefit from their services. Some clients only use the service when they make their RSP contributions— which may be only once or twice a year.

Myth #7 – There is no difference between a discount broker and a full-service investment dealer. To meet the needs of most investors, discount brokers provide access to the same investments as full-service brokers, but they do not give specific investment advice. When you use a discount broker to manage your own investments, you call a representative over the telephone to have your decisions carried out. You can also do this through your personal computer. You are able to transfer funds between accounts, get stock quotes, place buy and sell orders and get market information when it is convenient for you.

(Reprinted with permission from Royal Bank Action Direct— **www.actiondirect.com***)*

Financial Planning Basics for Discount Broker Clients

There's a glut of resources available for people who want to learn more about financial planning and investing basics, so much so that you could spend a lot of time just finding the right book or Web site. What follows is a brief look at some key financial concepts for discount broker clients. It's designed for people who want to use their brokerage account to build a balanced long-term investment portfolio. No, this stuff isn't as exciting as aggressive, speculative trading, but then most people don't aggressively trade their way to financial security.

Get Your Priorities Straight

One of the best ways to get you thinking about your financial priorities is to use a tool called the financial planning pyramid.

Figure 6: The Financial Planning Pyramid

SPECULATIVE OR VERY AGGRESSIVE	Art, IPOs, OTC securities, real estate, precious metals art and coins
AGGRESSIVE GROWTH	Tax shelters, commodities and derivatives
MODERATE GROWTH	Stocks and equity mutual funds
CONSERVATIVE GROWTH	Fixed income securities, GICs, and some mutual funds
SECURITY INDEPENDENCE	Life and disability insurance, will, power of attorney Debt, elimination, home, RRSPs emergency fund

The bottom of the pyramid represents the preservation of what you have already accumulated as opposed to building up your assets. In this analysis, it's more important to be properly insured than it is to have a stock portfolio or even an RRSP. Next on the list of priorities comes a combination of saving for life cycle events like retirement, as well as securing your financial security in the present by creating an emergency fund and eliminating debt. Paying off a credit card with a 17-per-cent interest rate will give you a lot more guaranteed bang for your buck than most investments.

Further up the pyramid, we come to asset-building through the purchase of stocks, bonds and mutual funds. At this level, Treasury bills, Canada Savings Bonds, guaranteed investment certificates and both federal and provincial government bonds would carry the least risk, while preferred and common stocks would entail greater risk. Still riskier are the investments at the top of the pyramid, things like over-the-counter (OTC) stocks, initial public offerings (IPOs), precious metals, real estate, then art and coins.

A lot of attention has been paid recently to successful IPOs, particularly those by technology companies traded on the Nasdaq stock market. Unfortunately, this has created the false impression that high returns are a sure thing when a company issues shares for the first time. Over-the-counter stocks refer to those start-ups that do not perhaps have the financial stability to make it to senior markets like the New York and Toronto stock exchanges. The risk in buying these stocks is considerable because many of them end up worthless. However, the benefits are potentially huge. For example, Bid.com International Inc. once traded on the Canadian over-the-counter market for pennies a share in an earlier incarnation as Internet Liquidators. It then graduated to the TSE and traded above $30 before falling back well below $10 at the end of 1999.

You can use the pyramid to help make sure all the financial planning bases are covered in your life and also as a guide to the level of risk associated with the various investment classes.

Investing Objectives

There are basically three objectives in investing: growth, otherwise known as capital appreciation, income and preservation of capital. A fourth could also be tax minimization.

Capital appreciation is determined by the growth of the value of certain securities. For example, if you were to buy 1,000 shares of a stock at $5 and later sell it for $15 you would have a $10/share capital gain. No tax would be payable until the security was sold, then only two-thirds of the gain would be subject to tax. In this case there was a $10,000 gain of which $6,666 would be taxable. Many people don't realize that a capital gain can occur from many securities including stocks, mutual funds and even bonds. Also, if you were to contribute assets to an RRSP a "deemed disposition" would be triggered and tax may be due.

Income can come from many places such as bond interest and from dividends paid by a corporation. Income paid by bonds are taxed at the marginal tax rate of the investor, while dividends benefit from the dividend tax credit. One dollar in dividends is "grossed up" by 25 per cent and then a tax credit of 13.3 per cent is applied.

Capital preservation is the third primary investment objective, whereby investors work hard to prevent their assets from being eroded by inflation. Even though they pay a relatively low level of income, GICs and T-bills are considered to be preservers of capital because in a market downturn their value remains essentially static.

A fourth goal—although not considered to be a primary motivation for investing—is tax minimization. This would include choosing investment vehicles that provide tax benefits such as a labour sponsored mutual fund.

Investor, Know Thyself

Take a look at all the questions about risk and objectives that are asked on the broker application form. Consider them as a way of gauging what kind of an investor you are. For instance, would you classify your risk tolerance as low, medium or high? And what are your objectives for your account? Long-term growth, income or a balanced approach?

The longer your investing horizon, the more risk you can afford to take on, and the more aggressive or growth-oriented you can be. On the other hand, if you're young but risk-averse, you'll want to swing more toward a balanced approach. The interesting thing about risk is that the more you take on, the higher your returns are likely to be in the long term. Of course, more risk also means a greater chance of losing money in the short term. So even though stocks have performed better than bonds over the years, there is a greater likelihood that at the end of any particular year that a stock portfolio would have lost money.

Risk, by the way, can broadly be defined as the possibility of not reaching your specific investment goals. In technical terms, the term risk refers to the volatility of a security's return compared to the overall market.

Asset Allocation

This is a fancy term meaning nothing more than the mix of the types of investments you'll use to reach your objective. In other words, it is the diversification of investment risks. The more conservative you are, the more of your assets you'll place in the fixed income category and the less you'll put into equities. Most asset allocation decisions are essentially stocks versus bonds, with a little cash thrown in to cover short-term emergencies or to enable you take advantage of buying opportunities.

The ultimate goal of diversification is to achieve the highest possible returns with the lowest possible risk. Research has shown that the greatest factor in determining a portfolio's return is the asset mix, accounting for between 80 and 90 per cent of the total return achieved. The rest is determined by specific security selection and market timing, which some cynics may say is more luck than anything else. A very simple guideline for determining the equity weighting in your portfolio is to subtract your age from 100. A 30-year-old might then have 70 per cent of her portfolio in stocks, while a 70-year-old would have 30 per cent.

Your time horizon—the amount of time you have before you need the money in your portfolio—will have a bearing on your asset allocation as well. You may be 30 but planning to dip into your investments to buy a house in a year. In that case, it would be wise to minimize your exposure to equities. The same goes if you are retired and dependant on the income derived from your investments to maintain a certain lifestyle.

Remember when deciding on your asset allocation that there's more to risk than the vagaries of the stock market. For instance, there's inflation. If you earn a six-per-cent return at a time when the inflation rate is three per cent, your real return is just three per cent. A good way to achieve a healthy long-term real return is to aim for five percentage points above the inflation rate.

Asset allocation is crucially important for discount broker-age clients because there's no supervision of your account by financial professionals. No one is going to say: "You should reduce your exposure to equities since you're saving for a down payment on a house." Nor will a discounter intrude into your personal life and suggest that you set up a regular investment plan so that you can build up your assets. A discounter will, on the other hand, step in if you order a security that entails risk beyond the tolerance you specified in your account application.

Building a Portfolio

A standard financial planning axiom is "pay yourself first," which means putting aside a set portion of your salary for investing. This philosophy was popularized by the wildly successful book *The Wealthy Barber*,* which suggests you can live comfortably by investing 10 percent of your earnings. But 10 percent may or may not be right for you—what's important is the concept of building a long-term portfolio by investing consistently. Consistently doesn't just mean on a regular basis, say every month or quarter. It also means taking a steady approach where you don't engage in the pointless exercise of market timing or jumping in and out of the market.

Peter Lynch, a renowned one-time portfolio manager at Fidelity Investments, has said that most investors in his fund had negative returns on investment. Why? Not because he was a bad fund manager. In fact, his fund was an anomaly in that it managed to consistently outperform the market. The problem for many investors in the fund was that they bought and sold too often instead of taking a buy-and-hold strategy. In effect, their moves meant they bought high and sold low.

If your investing goal is to save for retirement or to build up long-term gains, try to ignore the allure of the market and the impulse to start trading for trading's sake. Take the slow-and-steady approach and leave the speculating to a separate investing account that will allow you to have some fun.

Web Resources for Learning More about General Investing

When it comes to learning more about investing and personal finance, the World Wide Web is like a well-stocked library. Any of the major search engines will turn up dozens and dozens of sites on a particular financial subject. What we've done here is list some of the best along with a short explanation of what they offer.

---

* David B. Chilton, *The Wealthy Barber: Everyone's Common Sense Guide to Becoming Financially Independent*, Toronto: Stoddart, 1989.

www.aaii.com (American Association of Individual Investors): You have to be a paying member to gain access to some of the material on this site, but there are still lots of free articles worth reading. Recent examples: How Many Mutual Funds Should you Hold in Your Portfolio and The Cost of Panic Selling in Stock Market Investing. (a US site)

www.armchairmillionaire.com (Armchair Millionaire): Articles, message boards and on-line chats on all kinds of basic investing topics. Material is divided into getting started, savvy investor and fund-amentals (meaning mutual fund) categories. (US)

www.canadianfinance.com (Canadian Financial Network): Do a search on a financial topic and this site will produce a list of links with Canadian sites specially noted. (A Canadian site)

www.nucleus.com/wealthnet (Canada WealthNet): A collection of links to other investing sites. Stock exchanges, fund companies, financial advisors and financial news sites are included. (Cdn)

www.finpipe.com (Financial Pipeline): An amateurish-looking site that is well worth visiting for basic, unbiased information on basic investing subjects like how bonds and derivatives work. (Cdn)

www.imoney.com (imoney): This investing/personal finance site has a fairly large library of articles on investing and stock market basics. Lots of portfolio tracking and graphing tools for stocks and funds. (Cdn)

www.invest-faq.com (The Investment FAQ): Frequently-asked investing questions listed under topics like technical analysis and derivatives. (US)

www.investorlearning.ca (Investor Learning Centre): This site is the place to start for investing basics. The glossary provides concise, simple to understand definitions. (Cdn)

www.justquotes.com (Just Quotes): This superb stock research site also has a FAQ section with headings in such areas as bonds, derivatives, exchanges and so on.

www.moneysense.ca: *MoneySense* magazine's Web site has a big archive of articles in the current as well as previous issues, as well as other topics and features.

www.personalwealth.com (Standard & Poor's): Lots of material on investing basics, plus coverage of daily market action, ratings by S&P analysts and more. Some of the resources are only available to paying subscribers. (US)

www.teachmefinance.com (Teach Me Finance): Ultra-basic explanations of investing topics like bond valuations, annuities and interest rates. (US)

www.tickertalks.com (Tickertalks): Articles and commentary on all kinds of investing subjects. Includes interviews with investing figures. (Cdn)

2

The Players

There are 12 discount brokers in Canada and all but three—
E*Trade Canada, Charles Schwab and Sunlife Securities—are
owned by big financial institutions with a retail banking network. This means there's a very good chance that you'll be able
to set up an account at a discount broker that's in the same corporate family as your bank. Sure, it's convenient to do this, but
should you do that without first shopping around? We emphati-
cally say no. All discount brokers offer essentially the same thing
in giving you cheap access to the markets, but there remain big
differences in the amenities and level of service they offer and
their pricing of equity and mutual fund commissions.

What follows is a brief introduction to the 12 discounters.
Exhaustive comparative information appears through this book,
but here we've tried to help you get a general feel for which broker might be best for you. Note that discounters are constantly
updating their services and products. Always check your broker's
Web site for the latest information.

Bank of Montreal InvestorLine

Owner: Bank of Montreal

Established: 1988

Target Audience: From aggressive investors to those investing with a goal like retirement in mind

Web Address: www.investorline.com

Toll-Free Phone Number: 1-800-387-7800

E-Mail: info@investorline.com

Web Trading: Yes (called On-line Broker)

Phone Trading: Yes

Automated Phone Trading: Yes

InvestorLine is one of the larger players in the Canadian discount business and it offers a well-rounded range of services that will appeal to all types of investors. One way in which InvestorLine differs from everyone else and is that it offers a lower minimum commission for market orders ($25) than it does for limit orders ($29). It's a common pricing tactic among US discounters, but InvestorLine is one of only two Canadian brokers to do it (Disnat the other). Another unique feature at InvestorLine is the Account Link Service, which turns your brokerage account into a high interest chequing account with debit card access. Like many other discounters, InvestorLine has committed to introducing on-line bond trading this year. It also plans to upgrade its research tools and news offering.

Charles Schwab Canada

Owner: Charles Schwab Corporation of San Francisco

Established: 1999

Target Audience: The more affluent end of the business, including people who are looking for advice.

Web Address: www.schwabcanada.com

Toll-Free Phone Number: 1-888-597-9999 (in Toronto: 416-359-1900)

E-Mail: Service@SchwabCanada.com

Web Trading: Yes

Phone Trading: Yes

Automated Phone Trading: Yes (called TeleBroker)

Schwab is the top name in the US discount brokerage business and it has been for more than a decade. It made the jump into the Canadian market in February 1999, when it bought tiny Porthmeor Securities and Priority Brokerage.

Schwab signals its high-end aspirations by rejecting accounts with assets of less than $20,000. In fact, Schwab calls itself a full-choice broker not a discount broker. Clients can trade on their own, or work with an advisor who is paid with a salary and bonus, not through commissions tied to the investments he or she sells to clients. As you'd expect, you pay substantially higher commissions when you use Schwab's advisory services (the minimum equity commission is $100). Schwab's minimum on-line commission for self-traders is $30, which is a tick higher than other discounters.

You can't accuse Schwab of not providing value for its fees, though. There's an excellent collection of research tools, an IPO centre (**www.canadaIPO.com**), free Microsoft Money software and wireless trading through Bell Mobility digital PCS phones.

CIBC Investor's Edge

Owner: Canadian Imperial Bank of Commerce

Established: 1991

Target Audience: Broad range of investors with the time, knowledge and inclination to run their own portfolios

Web Address: www.investorsedge.cibc.com

Toll-Free Phone Number: 1-800-567-3343 (in Toronto: 416-980-3343)

E-Mail Address: isinewaccount.mailbox@cibc.ca

Web Trading: Yes (electronic services are called EdgeLine)

Phone Trading: Yes

Automated Phone Trading: Yes; voice recognition planned for mid-2000 (EdgeLine)

Investor's Edge has the makings of a good service for the masses, including 24 hour broker-assisted trading, access to global stock markets, zero commissions on front-end mutual funds and a new voice-activated telephone trading system. The problem is in the packaging. At the time this book was published, Investor's Edge had a third-rate Web site that was laughably out of date in its appearance and the information and services it offered.

We're betting that the Investor's Edge Web site will have had a make-over by the time you read this. You can also expect a number of other improvements in service including e-mail trade confirmations and new on-line resources for researching stocks.

CT Securities

Owner: Canada Trust

Established: 1995

Target Audience: Investors seeking an extra level of service unavailable at other discounters

Web Address: www.ctsecurities.com

Toll-Free Phone Number: 1-800-560-6373 (in Toronto: 416-863-6373) (in Quebec: 1-877-281-1654) (in Montreal: 514-281-1654)

Web Trading: Yes

Phone Trading: Yes

Automated Phone Trading: Coming in 2000

How much longer CT Securities will be around is anyone's guess. With Toronto-Dominion Bank having bought CT parent Canada Trust, it's only a matter of time until CT Securities clients are folded into the TD Waterhouse's operation. CT is actually positioned a little differently than TD in the discount marketplace. CT considers itself a "value-added brokerage," which it describes as a step up from a discount broker. An example of this extra level of service is that clients have access to trading professionals rather than just broker/order-takers. CT says its traders will make a special effort to help clients get a better price on their orders. The thinking is that active traders would rather shave a nickel or dime off the bid/asked rather than go to a cheaper broker and save $5 on the commission.

Though its equity commissions are on the high side, CT was a leader in eliminating front-load commissions on mutual funds in the discount business. It was also the first to provide in-house research reports to clients at no cost, although generally its research tools have been nothing to get excited about.

Disnat

Owner: Le Mouvement des caisses Desjardins

Established: 1982

Target Audience: A broad range of do-it-yourself investors

Web Address: www.disnat.com

Toll-Free Phone Number: 1-800-268-8471 (in Montreal: 514-842-2685)

E-Mail: information.disnat@riq.qc.ca

Web Trading: Yes

Phone Trading: Yes

Automated Phone Trading: No

Disnat was Canada's first discount broker, believe it or not. That's no slight on Disnat, only a reflection of the fact that this dealer is focused on the Quebec market and so no presence in the rest of Canada. Disnat is the number one player in Quebec, although National Bank Discount Brokerage says it's close behind. Disnat offers a reasonably good package, although its Web site is looking a little on the ragged side. If you're looking for state-of-the-art tools for researching stocks and funds and keeping up with market news, you won't find them here.

E*Trade Canada

Owner: VERSUS Brokerage Services Inc.

Established: 1997

Target Audience: Well-informed, net-savvy investors who make their own investing decisions.

Web Address: www.canada.etrade.com

Toll-Free Phone Number: 1-888-872-3388 (in Toronto: 416-214-6457)

E-Mail: service@tradeit.com

Web Trading: Yes (called E*Station)

Phone Trading: Yes

Automated Phone Trading: Yes (called Tele*Master)

E*Trade is Canada's one true on-line broker. Almost 90 per cent of its trades are done on the Web, compared to around two-thirds at most others. There's are also no branch offices that E*Trade clients can visit.

E*Trade parent VERUS Brokerage has licensed the E*Trade name from the US company E*Trade Group Inc. of Palo Alto, California. In the United States, E*Trade is one of the larger discount brokers, but in Canada, it is a very small player. E*Trade's difficulties building market share are partly a result of the fact that it hasn't differentiated itself much from the other players in Canada. In the United States, on-line brokers generally operate at the low end of the commission scale. In Canada, E*Trade isn't notably cheaper than everyone else. E*Trade runs a very user-friendly electronic operation, although there have been complaints that it lacks the resources necessary to provide a good telephone trading option for clients.

E*Trade offers a free 60-day trial in which you can test its on-line tools and services (though you can't trade).

HSBC InvestDirect

Owner: HSBC Bank Canada

Established: 1995

Target Audience: Knowledgeable clients with at least $10,000 in assets; also, people with an interest in trading on foreign stock markets, particularly Hong Kong

Web Address: www.hsbcinvestdirect.com

Toll-Free Phone Number: 1-800-398-1180 (in Toronto: 416-868-6800; in Vancouver: 604-641-1180)

E-Mail Address: support1@hsbc-netTRADER.com

Web Trading: Yes (called netTrader)

Phone Trading: Yes

Automated Phone Trading: No

InvestDirect is part of the Canadian subsidiary (formerly known here as Hong Kong Bank of Canada) of the London-based HSBC global banking business. HSBC has extensive interests in the Far East, so InvestDirect has a particularly strong market share among people of Asian background.

Not surprisingly, InvestDirect offers far greater access to international markets than most other discounters. You can place trades on all major markets in Europe and Asia, including Hong Kong, Japan, China, Singapore, Australia, England, Germany, France and Italy. InvestDirect even offers on-line trading on the Hong Kong market. The global orientation of this discounter extends into the news and research it offers as well. For example, it offers free access to market news from over 20 global news services and news release services, including Agence France Press, Asia Info Services and Xinhua.

National Bank Discount Brokerage

Owner: National Bank of Canada

Established: 1988

Target Audience: A broad range of self-directed investors, with a special effort made to serve those with an interest in mutual funds

Web Address: www.invesnet.com

Toll-Free Phone Number: 1-800-363-3511 (in Montreal: 514-866-6755)

E-Mail: support@invesnet.com

Web Trading: Yes

Automated Phone Trading: Yes

National Bank's fast-growing discount business used to have some identity problems. Its phone service was called InvesTel, but that name was de-emphasized as the on-line service, called InvesNet, became popular. Then in late 1999, the whole operation was given a new, clearer title: National Bank Discount Brokerage. Along with the name change, this discounter also made a major investment to ugrade its Web site.

Though primarily a player in Quebec, National Bank's service will be of interest to cost-conscious investors in all of the six provinces in which it operates (the exceptions are the Prairie provinces and Newfoundland). Whereas most players charge in the $27 to $29 range as a minimum commission, National Bank has a $24.50 floor price. As well, National Bank has no fees for its self-directed RRSP and RESP.

Royal Bank Action Direct

Owner: Royal Bank of Canada

Established: 1989

Target Audience: Self-managed investors generally, but more focused on higher net-worth individuals making all or some of their own investing decisions

Web Address: www.actiondirect.com

Toll-Free Phone Number: 1-877-977-0677

E-Mail: Available through the "contact us" button on the Web site

Web Trading: Yes (called NetAction)

Phone Trading: Yes

Automated Phone Trading: Yes (called TelAction)

Not as big as TD Waterhouse, Action Direct is still an industry giant. Call it a friendly giant. If you visit the Action Direct Web site, you'll see a pleasant, well-organized presentation that speaks to

all kinds of investors. For instance, the home page has prominently displayed links to the Action Direct Education Centre and
to the Fund Network, a package of services aimed at the mutual
fund crowd. For serious equity investors, it offers extensive
research tools and Canadian and US market news culled from 10
different sources.

Action Direct is on the pricier side in equity commissions,
although front-end loads have been eliminated on mutual fund
accounts larger than $15,000. Action Direct also offers a full
range of electronic services, including an alternative to Web trading called PCAction that allows your computer to dial directly
into the Action Direct computer system.

Scotia Discount Brokerage

Owner: Bank of Nova Scotia

Established: 1984

Target Audience: Knowledgeable investors looking for low fees.

Web Address: www.sdbi.com

Toll-Free Phone Number: 1-800 263-3430

E-Mail: sdbi_tor@sdbi.com

Web Trading: Yes (called StockLine)

Phone Trading: Yes

Automated Phone Trading: Yes

Scotia stepped away from the pack on pricing in 1998 and
nobody followed. This means that if you're looking for rock-
bottom commissions, then you have to consider Scotia. Consider it carefully, though. It's commission structure means
you'll pay less for some trades and more for others—especially
those over $2,000. As well, you'll find this broker offers little in
the way of amenities. It has one of the more spartan Web sites
around and it offers few research or on-line tools.

Scotia's marketing strategy has been to go after savvy active
traders looking to minimize commissions. However, they have
recently tried to attract the conservative, long-term mutual fund
investor by offering rebates on purchases of mutual funds with
a deferred sales charge.

Sun Life Securities

Owner: Sun Life Assurance Co. of Canada

Established: 1995

Target Audience: Sun Life insurance clients, novice investors

Web Address: www.sunsecurities.com

Toll-Free Phone Number: 1-800-835-0812 (in Toronto 416-408-797; in Montreal 514- 879-2040)

E-Mail: slsweb@sunlife.com

Web Trading: Yes

Phone Trading: Yes

Automated Phone Trading: No

Sun Life Securities started out by quietly marketing itself to Sun Life's insurance customer base rather than doing broad-based advertising. At the same time, however, Sun Life began laying the groundwork for a marketing twist that would help differentiate it from the other 11 players. Instead of casting a wide net for clients, Sun Life chose to put an emphasis on novices, or more specifically people who may never have bought a stock before. If you look at their Web site, you'll see it looks utterly non-threatening and has a big emphasis on investor learning. Lots of information on trading on-line is provided, and phone traders have been instructed to offer a higher then normal amount of assistance to clients.

While Sun Life's marketing strategy is bound to appeal to rookie investors, the firm's lack of amenties will make it less appealing to those with experience in the markets.

TD Waterhouse

Owner: Toronto-Dominion Bank

Established: 1984

Target Audience: Everyone

Web Address: www.tdwaterhouse.ca

Toll-Free Phone Number: 1-800-465-5463.

E-Mail: tdwaterhouse@tdbank.ca

Web Trading: Yes (called Web Broker)

Phone Trading: Yes

Automated Phone Trading: Yes (called TalkBroker)

The former Green Line is the king of discounters in Canada and a major player globally, with operations in the United States, the United Kingdom, Hong Kong and Australia. Waterhouse considers itself the discount brokerage equivalent of the big-box retailer, selling virtually every investing option imaginable. The strategy of being all things to all people is a tough one to do well, but Waterhouse manages it. Nobody offers more on-line research to its clients, and yet novices will find lots of basic information on the Web site about things like how to place a trade and how options work. Commissions are still on the higher wide, but the move to eliminate front-load mutual fund fees in 1999 was definitely a step in the right direction. As well, Waterhouse offers state-of-the-art technical services, including an automated phone trading system that uses voice recognition technology.

Toronto-Dominion Bank's amalgamation of Green Line with its US-based Waterhouse Securities operation has brought some new ideas and products to the Canadian operation. Still, it looked at least initially like the US service offered by Waterhouse had a few more perks for clients. Do your own comparison by visiting Waterhouse's American Web site at: www.tdwater-house.com.

And look out for eNorthern, a new electronic brokerage. Unlike other on-line brokers, eNorthern's operation—at **www.enorthern.com**—will provide a wide range of on-line financial services, from IPOs and securities trading to private placements and commercial mortgages.

Web Resources for Comparing Discount Brokers

www.bay-street.com (Bay-Street.com): This very good Canadi-an investing site includes a short but useful review of the ser-vices and commissions at nine discounters. A similar summary of major US discounters is there as well. Warning: If you think Canadian discount broker commissions are too high, don't read the information about the US deep discounter Datek On-line and its US$9.99 commissions.

www.ndir.com (Directions): A must-see all-around investing site that has kept a detailed section on discount brokers for sev-eral years now. There are commission comparisons, a survey of Web site speed at major discounters, an option and equity com-mission calculator and a look at US discounters.

www.quicken.ca (Quicken): The brokerage centre on this all-purpose investing and personal finance site is a good place to start comparison shopping for discounters. There are hyperlinks to the Web sites of all 12 discount brokers, plus articles on sub-jects like using a US discount broker, and how to tell whether you should use a full-service broker or a discounter. The best feature is an on-line calculator that allows you to type in your trading habits (e.g., phone or on-line, frequency of trades) and then tells you which broker would offer the cheapest commissions.

3

Getting Started

Once you have selected the discount broker that is right for you, the next step is to set up an account. This sounds simple but it's actually a fairly involved process. First, you have to decide what type of account you want. Then, you have to fill out an account application that's a lot more detailed and complex than you'd probably imagine. In this chapter, we explain the various types of accounts and then take you through the application form step by step. There are five steps in the process:

Step One: Pick the Kind of Account You Want

Step Two: Getting an Application Form

Step Three: Filling Out the Form

Step Four: On-line Set-up

Step Five: Putting Cash in Your Account

Step One: Pick the Kind of Account You Want

The Cash Account

This most basic account comes in either a Canadian- or US-dollar version and allows you to buy a wide range of investments, with the notable exception of options. You also can't buy on margin with a cash account and you can't short sell. All purchases must be paid in full in cash on settlement of the trade, which in the case of stocks is three business days. Buy 100 shares of a $25 stock and you will be expected to pay $2,500 plus commissions. By default, all accounts are cash accounts unless otherwise specified.

The Margin Account

This type of account allows you to take a loan from the broker to cover part of the cost of buying securities. The loan is secured by other securities that you own or by the stocks you're buying. Since lending is involved, a credit check is always part of the application process.

The term margin refers to the amount of money put up by the investor, while the amount lent by the broker is called the debit balance. The size of loan your broker will give you depends on the cost and type of security you're buying, but the usual range is between 30 and 70 per cent of the value of the holding itself. Although securities regulators do allow margin for stocks that trade at less than $3, most brokers use that as a minimum. The brokers also won't offer margin for stocks that trade on the Canadian Venture Exchange and the Canadian Dealing Network. In addition to stocks, you can buy mutual funds, GICs and bonds on margin.

The risk in margin investing is that you'll face a margin call. This happens when the value of your securities falls and the margin you originally provided no longer meets the minimum requirement. Then, you must increase the amount of money you put down to buy your securities.

Here's a simple example of how margin works. Say you buy 1,000 shares of a $10 stock that has a maximum loan value of 70 per cent. If you wanted, you could buy those shares by putting down only $3,000 or 30 per cent of the transaction. Margin also works in connection with the value of the securities in your account. If you chose to pay in full for those 1,000 shares, your broker would then allow you to borrow $7,000 based on the value of the equities in your account. Your broker might tell you in this case that your purchasing power is $7,000. When the value of the stock rises, so does your purchasing power. Purchasing power can be reduced by what's known as a buffer, or pillow, which means your broker won't lend you quite as much as you might technically be able to borrow. The idea is to protect you from an immediate margin call should the value of your portfolio fall.

Be advised that your broker may limit the margin available to you, or not allow you any at all, if your holdings are too concentrated. That can mean you hold only a small number or even a single stock in your portfolio, or you're over-weighted in a sector, such as high-tech.

Broker interest rates for margin loans are quite competitive, usually just a percentage point above the major banks' prime lending rate. For this reason, buying on margin is an attractive alternative to a plain investment loan or using your line of credit. As with most loans used to generate investing gains, interest paid on a margin loan is tax-deductible.

A margin account is also required for options trading and short selling, a strategy in which you try to profit from a stock's short-term price decline. In simple terms, you borrow the shares from your broker and then sell them in the hope you can replace them at a lower price later on. Short selling is available at all discounters, but like options it's generally reserved for clients who have a certain level of expertise.

Canadian regulators require that certain margin standards be adhered to although individual brokers can, and do, impose higher standards.

Below are the maximum loan values for Canadian and US stock exchange stock list.

	Per cent of Market Value
Option Eligible	70%
>= $2.00	50%
>= $1.75 to $1.99	40%
>= $1.50 to $1.74	20%
< $1.50	no loan value

By virtue of the criteria for a stock to be option eligible it must trade above $5.00 as well as meeting other standards.

Figure 1: Margin Requirements at a typical discount broker, in this case Action Direct

Security	Margin Required	Loan Value
Stocks		
Canadian Option Eligible*	30%	70%
Option Eligible S&P 500 Index	30%	70%
US Option Eligible	40%	60%
$5 and over	50%	50%
$3 to $4.99	75%	25%
Rights and Warrants		
$5 and over	50%	50%
$3 to $5.99	75%	25%
Debt		
Corporate bonds and debentures	20%	80%
Municipal bonds	20%	80%
GICs	20%	80%
Provincial bonds	10%	90%
Corporate paper	10%	90%
Government of Canada or US bonds	7%	93%
Government of Canada Treasury bills	3%	97%
Mutual Funds	50%	50%

* a stock that satisfies certain requirements for liquidity, market capitalization and so on.

Figure 2: Margin Interest Rates

Bank of Montreal InvestorLine	prime + 1%
Charles Schwab	prime + 2% for < $5,000; prime + 1.5% $5,000 to $10,000; prime + 1% $10,001 to $50,000; prime + .5% $50,001 to $100,000; prime > $100,000
CIBC Investor's Edge	prime +2% <$10,000; prime + 1.5% $10,000 to $50,000; prime +1%> $50,000
CT Securities	prime +1%
Disnat	prime +1%
E*Trade	prime
HSBC InvesDirect	prime +1%
National Bank InvesNet/Investel	prime +1%
Royal Bank Action Direct	prime + 1%
Scotia Discount Brokerage	prime +1% <$ 25,000; prime + .5% >$25,000
Sun Life Securities	prime +1.5%<$50,000; prime +1% >$50,000
TD Waterhouse	prime +1%

Registered Accounts

Discount brokerage accounts are often thought of as tools for aggressive stock traders, but they also make a good home for the more conservative investing that goes along with registered retirement savings plans (RRSPs) and registered retirement income funds (RRIFs).

Lots of investors have scattered RRSP accounts at several different banks, mutual fund companies and insurers, which is both a record-keeping nightmare and bad money management. The federal government allows Canadians to invest a limited portion of their retirement accounts outside Canada, but the limit applies to each individual plan and not the aggregate. If you have lots of little RRSPs, you can only invest a portion of each internationally. The solution is to group everything together in a self-directed plan at a discounter. Not only will you get more bang for your foreign investing buck, you'll also have the benefit of being able to choose from a wide selection of investing choices. Consolidating your accounts will also save you from having to pay several different annual RRSP or RRIF administration fees. If you have less than $15,000 to $25,000 in a discount brokerage RRSP and RRIF account, you'll pay anywhere from $25 to $100 per year, but if your account is larger, you'll pay no annual administration fees. It's also worth noting that some discounters offer RRSPs with no annual fee on small-size accounts, providing they are placed in a limited range of investments that usually comprises GICs and mutual funds. If you can't find a no-cost account like this at your discounter and you have only a few thousand dollars in assets, then paying an annual administration fee may be prohibitively expensive.

Discounters charge the annual administration fee on smaller retirement accounts because of the paperwork involved. To start with, each RRSP has to be registered with the Canada Customs and Revenue Agency. After that, contributions and foreign content levels have to be regularly reported to the tax people. If someone withdraws some money from an RRSP or deregisters a plan, that creates additional paperwork. Deregistration of your RRSP will be taxed as income in the year the money is withdrawn at your marginal tax rate. The holding institution is required to withhold tax when deregistering the plan at the following rates.

RRSP Withholding Taxes Rates		
Amount Withdrawn	Percentage Withheld All provinces except Quebec	(Quebec)
<$5,000	10%	21%
$5,000 < $15,000	20%	30%
>$15,000	30%	35%

RRSP administration fees can have a large impact on your net returns, so do your homework before opening an RRSP account. Let's say you had an RRSP with a discounter whose annual administration charge was $100. If your account at the beginning of the year was, say $2,000 and you earned a respectable 10 per cent return, at the end of the year your portfolio was worth $2,200. But this does not take into account the $100 fee paid from your own pocket that would reduce your returns by half, putting you in the return range of a GIC with much more risk. You would probably have been better off investing with a mutual fund company directly or with your local bank which likely wouldn't charge you anything. Or, you could choose the discounters with the lowest admin fees like HSBC or National bank with a $0 fee or BMO, Disnat and Action Direct who maintain a $25 fee.

Figure 3: RRSP Administration Fees

Broker	Annual Fee (GST Extra)	Fee Waived After Account Reaches
Bank of Montreal InvestorLine	$25	$25,000
Charles Schwab	none	minimum account of $20,000
CIBC Investor's Edge	$100	$15,000
CT Securities	$100	$25,000
Disnat	$25	$25,000
E*Trade Canada	$38.88	$20,000
HSBC InvestDirect	none	—
National Bank Discount Brokerage	none	—
Royal Bank Action Direct	$25	$25,000
Scotia Discount Brokerage	$75	$15,000
Sun Life	$95	$15,000
TD Waterhouse	$100	$25,000
(Note: RRIF fees are generally the same as RRSP fees but check with your broker.)		

If you're setting up a Spousal RRSP account, then you'll have to provide your spouse's social insurance number. Either spouse may contribute to the plan, so be sure to tell your discounter who's making the contribution so the contributor can get the tax benefit. One of the obvious benefits to spousal RRSPs is the income splitting potential for those couples in which one spouse has an income that is substantially higher than the other. You should also be aware that any withdrawal from a Spousal RRSP made within three years of the contribution would be taxed in the hands of the spousal contributor regardless of who made the withdrawal.

What about buying and selling stocks within your RRSP of companies that don't trade on an exchange—those referred to as a Canadian Controlled Private Corporations? As the name implies, CCPCs are Canadian corporations that do not trade publicly on an exchange. There may be restrictions but many qualify as RRSP eligible and can be held with your discounter. You would want to provide audited financial statements for the company indicating its fair market value for RRSP purposes. However, at many discounters the cost involved to have the shares deposited to your account can be prohibitively expensive. Some, for example, will charge $300 just to receive them into the account and then a quarterly or annual administration fee as well.

RRIF Basics

Just about everyone knows about RRSPs, but RRIFs aren't understood as well. If you have an RRSP, you'll have to collapse it at the end of the year in which you turn 69 years of age. The choices are to cash it out (but then all of your RRSP assets will be taxed as income in that year), buy an annuity (a possibility that is right for many people) or transfer the assets to a RRIF.

Most of the same assets can be held in the RRIF as in RRSP, so transferring your assets is not too complicated. Most people open RRIFs at age 69 but, there is no minimum age at which to start one. You must, however, make regular withdrawals from RRIFs according to a schedule based on your age. These minimum withdrawals are based on a formula—$1/(90 -age)$. So if the investor was 65 and wished to draw on the RRIF in conjunction with Canada Pension Plan payments then he or she would receive $1/(90 - 65)$ or $1/25$ or 4 per cent of the portfolio. From the age of 69, the mandatory annual withdrawal is 4.76 per cent of the portfolio's balance as at Dec 31 of the previous year, and once you reach the age of 94, 20 per cent of the portfolio must be redeemed annually. RRIF and RRSP withdrawals are taxed as income in the hands of the annuitant. If a RRIF is transferred from one institution to another, the transferring institution is responsible for that year's payment.

Once the account is set up and a redemption is required, you can choose which assets to sell first—i.e., sell money market funds, then your equities, and you can withdraw any amount you want from a RRIF. You may convert your RRIF to an annuity, but not vice versa. An annuity is a contract with a financial institution that guarantees to pay a regular income for a specified length of time or until the death of the individual or person's spouse.

Figure 4: RRIF Payout Schedule

	Percentage of Total To Be Paid Out Annually	
Age as of Dec. 31	Before Dec. 31/ 92	After Dec. 31/92
69	4.76	4.76
70	5.00	5.00
71	5.26	7.38
72	5.56	7.48
73	5.88	7.59
74	6.25	7.71
75	6.67	7.85
76	7.14	7.99
77	7.69	8.15
78	8.33	8.33
79	8.53	8.53
80	8.75	8.75
81	8.99	8.99
82	9.27	9.27
83	9.58	9.58
84	9.93	9.93
85	10.33	10.33
86	10.79	10.79
87	11.33	11.33
88	11.96	11.96
89	12.71	12.71
90	13.62	13.62
91	14.73	14.73

Locked-In Accounts

Locked-in accounts are ones in which pension funds have been transferred from some other plan such as a collapsed company pension. In this type of account the funds held within it are protected and "locked-in" under pension legislation until the annuitant reaches a certain age. 'Locked-in' plans can also include LIFs (life income funds), and LRIFs (life retirement income funds), but each has its own specific characteristics. Generally the locked-in plans refer to federally regulated pension plans regardless of the province in which the plan was set up, however, BC, Nova Scotia, PEI and the Territories also have LRSPs (locked-in RSPs) which function in the same way.

LIRAs (locked-in retirement accounts) are very similar in nature to the LRSPs above but are governed by provincial legislation. The funds are locked in according to the provincial regulations until such time as the annuitant reaches a certain age (usually 65) at which time they can purchase a life annuity or a LIF. Most provinces offer LIRAs including Alberta, Saskatchewan, Manitoba, Ontario, Quebec, New Brunswick and Newfoundland.

A LIF (life income fund) can only be opened with funds transferred from an existing LIRA or LRSP, but once a LIF is opened the annuitant can make withdrawals in the same manner as those from a RRIF. One difference is that there is also a maximum withdrawal allowed from the plan which is designed so that there will be an income from which the annuitant can live off, depending on life expectancy. As with RRIFs the minimum annual withdrawal = value of plan / (90 - age of customer). This is used up to the age of 70; after that the following percentage method is used until age 80 when the person would purchase a life annuity.

Minimum Withdrawals from LIFs	
Age	**Per Cent**
71	7.38
72	7.48
73	7.59
74	7.71
75	7.85
76	7.99
77	8.15
78	8.33
79	8.53
80	8.75

RESP ACCOUNTS: Registered Education Savings Plans allow parents to save money for their children's education while deferring taxes. They were a niche product in the investing world until the 1998 federal budget made them more attractive. It took awhile for discounters to wake up to the new market, but now many of them offer self-directed RESPs. From an investing standpoint, these work much the same as RRSPs. The parent administering the plan and making contributions can choose from a wide range of investments, mixing them up in a way that would be impossible in an RESP from a bank or other financial institution because they would only sell-inhouse mutual funds and GICs.

Figure 5: Brokers Offering Self-Directed RESPs

Administration Fees	
Broker	**Annual Administration Fee (GST extra)**
Charles Schwab Canada	none
Disnat	TBA
National Bank Discount Brokerage	none
Royal Bank Action Direct	$25
Scotia Discount Brokerage	$25
Sun Life Securities	none
TD Waterhouse	$50 (waived if you have an RRSP, RRIF, Focus RRSP and Focus RRIF account as well)

(Note: RESP accounts are being added and changed all the time, so do your homework. Check especially with the brokers not listed here.)

Within an RESP a parent or guardian can contribute up to $4,000 per year for each child to a $42,000 total, but the standard rule of thumb is $2,000 per year for 21 years. At that rate, the federal Canada Education Savings Grant (CESG) will provide a

matching 20 per cent contribution up to $400 per year, for a life-
time total of $7,200. If the child chooses not to continue their
post-secondary education right away, that's no problem. Contributions to the plan must cease at age 21, but the plan does not
have to be collapsed until the last day of the 25th year following
the year in which the plan was opened. You can change the beneficiary of the plan.

The investments in the plan compound tax-free, and when
collapsed, the plan's investment gains are taxed in the hands of
the student, who is presumably in a low tax bracket. There are no
restrictions on how much of the plan can be invested internationally. If the child does not attend a qualifying post-secondary
institution, then up to $50,000 in the plan can be rolled into your
RRSP, depending on your contribution room. Otherwise, you
must withdraw the money in the plan and face a 20 per cent
penalty on the gains.

Make sure you have the child's/children's Social Insurance
Numbers. If you don't have the SINs then you may download the
application form from the Web site of Human Resources Development Canada (www.hrdc-drhc.gc.ca), or obtain a paper form
at an HRDC office. Be careful, as well, to indicate whether the
account is to be a family plan where many names can be provided or an individual plan for only one child.

Figure 6: RESP Growth

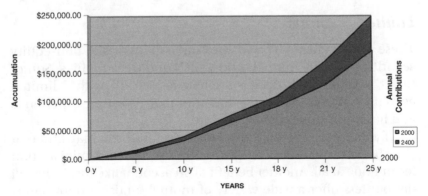

As you will notice the accumulation levels off in the Year 21 because RESP rules dictate that a maximum of $42,000 be contributed to the fund (an average of $2,000 for 21 years). As well, in Year 18 the RESP will reach its maximum $7,200 Canada Education Savings Grant (18 x $400 = $7,200). There's an ongoing debate about whether RESPs or in-trust accounts are a better vehicle for saving money to put toward a child's post-secondary education. The biggest point in favour of RESPs is that the federal government's Canada Education Savings Grant will match up to 20 per cent of your annual contribution to an maximum of $400 per year.

With an informal in-trust account, you have no worries about whether the child goes to university or not, but you forfeit the chance to collect what could over the years amount to thousands in government grant money. One way to settle the debate is to contribute $2,000 to an RESP to take maximum advantage of the grant, then contribute the rest to a trust account.

One of the strategies that has emerged to help investors decide where and how to invest when advisors push and pull them in many directions is to invest as much to their RRSP as they can. If they can invest enough to earn a $2,000 tax return that would be used to purchase an RESP for the child. The government then contributes the 20 per cent Canada Education Savings Grant, up to $400 per year.

Limited Accounts

These are for clients who wish to trade in less-risky, non-equity securities, usually mutual funds, GICs and treasury bills. Sometimes, a broker will decide a client is best off with a limited account because he or she has minimal investing experience and has never bought stocks before.

If you use a limited account for your RRSP, you may find that your broker will either charge a minimal annual administration fee or none at all. Another benefit of an account like this is that all discounters offer a wide variety of mutual funds with low commissions, in many cases no commission at all. However, if you plan to buy funds only and not mix in fixed income investments, then you might be better off with one of the funds-only brokers that charge no commissions. E*Trade Canada is the only discount broker to have completely eliminated fund commissions.

Investment Club Accounts

This kind of account first appeared at full-service brokers, where investment advisers would provide analyst reports and suggestions to members of the club. Although not all discounters offer investment club accounts, those that do require that an investment club agreement be signed indicating who has trading authority, the names and occupations of all the members as well as who may have inside knowledge on the operations of publicly traded companies. A discounter may also require that a bank account be set up in the club's name at an affiliated bank.

There are two ways to set up an investment club, either as a corporation or as a partnership (technically a modified partnership in the eyes of Canada Customs and Revenue.) By far most investment clubs are set up as a modified partnership where each of the members owns a portion of the club in relation to the amount invested.

Let's say, for example, that there are 10 original members in a club that we'll call Bold Moves. Each original member's contribution of $500 would buy 100 units, each worth $5. Skip forward a month when the units have appreciated to $600 (an unrealistic figure but the members are making bold moves after all). Each unit is now worth $6, so as they proceed to contribute their agreed upon monthly contribution of $50, that $50 now buys only 9.3333 additional units. Any new members would be able to purchase units according to the contribution and the value of the units themselves.

The tax implications of such a group should be discussed with a tax professional, but essentially the members of the club own units of the holdings and taxes are assessed according to how many units a member owns.

Informal Trust Accounts

These accounts are typically used by parents who want to put aside some money for their children. The account is opened in a parent's name and held separate from the rest of his or her own personal investments. A key thing to be aware of with discount broker informal trust accounts is that they are not legal trusts. The distinction is an important one from a tax perspective, because with an informal trust, the parent who contributes the money faces the tax bill. A formal trust can usually be identified by the fact that there is a legal document saying the account does in fact belong to the child. The benefit of doing this is that the investment gains earned by the trust are taxed in the hands of the child who likely won't have to pay any tax at all.

Estate Accounts

If an account holder were to die, the discounter would be provided with a certified true copy of the will, the death certificate and a letter of direction detailing who will be trading the account. The benefit of doing this is that you can strategically liquidate the account rather than just selling out in one fell swoop.

Premium Accounts

If you're an active trader who generates commissions of at least $5,000 per year, or if you have a portfolio worth at least $250,000, your broker will probably offer you a premium account. At TD Waterhouse, for example, they call it the President's Account, and at HSBC InvestDirect it's the Priority Gold account. Behind the fancy names are a few benefits that are worth having. For instance, you may get access to a priority trading phone line that is staffed by more experienced brokers. As well, you should get reduced commissions and possibly an additional quarter of a percentage point worth of interest on your cash balances. Other benefits include free research reports or real-time stock quotes.

If you are a candidate for a premium account, talk to different brokers to see what they offer. You'll find them quite anxious for your business, as any full-service broker would be. Big clients are big money for brokers, both in terms of the commissions and the trailer fees they generate through their mutual fund holdings (trailer fees are paid by the fund company to the selling broker as compensation for continuing service to the client). Big clients also offset the costs of maintaining all those tiny accounts that never or rarely get used but still have to receive account statements every month.

Figure 7: Premium Accounts and What They Offer

Bank of Montreal InvestorLine
A new package for VIP clients is in the works.

Charles Schwab Canada
None

CIBC Investor's Edge
Premium Edge
Requires: $250,000 in assets and $6,000 in annual commissions
Gives You: Access to a dedicated investment representative, a dedicated phone line, eligibility for commission discounts.

CT Securities
None

Disnat
Commission discounts are available for heavy traders on a case-by-case basis.

E*Trade Canada
A new premium account package for active investors called Power E-Trade Canada is on its way.

HSBC InvestDirect
Priority Gold
Requires: $250,000 in assets or $6,000 in annual commissions
Gives You: A 5-per-cent commission reduction, reduced margin rates and higher credit balance rates; discounted research and trade alert services; 500 real-time quotes

Priority Platinum
Requires: $500,000 in assets or $12,000 in annual commissions
Gives You: A 10-per-cent commission reduction, unlimited real-time quotes, plus all priority gold benefits

National Bank Discount Brokerage
Requires: $500,000 in assets or $7,000 in annually commissions
Gives You: 10 per cent off commissions on trading through a representative; reduced borrowing rates; personalized service through a direct trading line and designated rep; cash management services; waived fees for transfers and account substitutions

---

Royal Bank Action Direct
Select Service
Requires: $250,000 in assets or $5,000 in annual commissions
Gives You: Lower equity commissions; higher interest rates paid on cash balances; priority telephone line answered by seasoned brokers

Scotia Discount Brokerage
Priority trading lines and discounted commissions are provided on an account by account basis. You have to ask about it.

Sun Life Securities
None

TD Waterhouse
President's Account (By invitation only)
Requires: The guideline is $5,000 in annual commissions.
Gives You: Exclusive use of a special team of investment representatives; monthly commission rebates; preferred interest rates on debit and credit balances; free chequing and bank machine access through a MoneyLink account; free access to on-line research

---

Corporate/Non-Personal Accounts

These are established for corporations, societies, trusts and so on. For corporate accounts, a discounter will require additional forms such as one for corporate trading authority, a guarantee form in which a principal of the company guarantees the firm's trading assets and also the articles of incorporation. Sole proprietorship accounts can also be accommodated generally with a separate form as can partnership accounts. In these cases the applicant, often the principal of the business, would provide information on the company as well as the principal.

Step Two: Getting an Application Form

If you plan to use one of the many discounters owned by a bank, the best way to get your account going is to walk into a branch and ask for an application. If you go to a regional main branch, it's quite likely you can ask to see a representative of the broker face-to-face. In some cases, regular branch staff have been briefed on how to help a client fill out the discount broker application form, but this isn't standard. You may just get a blank stare at some locations.

If you do happen to find a helpful branch representative, you should be able to leave the application with him or her so that it can be sent via inter-bank mail to the regional brokerage office. Some brokers may act on a faxed copy of the application with the originals to follow, which can speed the process along. You can also call your potential discount broker and ask for an application to be mailed to you, or you can send an e-mail request to a broker via its Web site. Most broker Web sites also allow you to download the account application form. For this, you'll need a free software program called an Adobe Acrobat Reader. If you don't have one, download it from the Adobe Web site (www.adobe.com). Once you've printed the forms, fill them out, sign them and then either bring them to a branch or mail them to the address listed on the Web site. If speed is a concern, go to a branch. You'll have to use the mail in the case of E*Trade Canada since it's strictly an electronic outfit with no branches.

TD Waterhouse and Scotia Discount Brokerage are among the brokers that have created an on-line sign-up process where you fill out a form on the Web site and then transmit it to head office over the Internet. Even if you do send the form electronically, you still have to fill out a paper account form, sign it and then send it along. Printed documents will never be replaced in the account set-up process because your broker must have a copy of your signature on file.

Step Three: Filling Out the Form

First, be sure you've got the right forms for the account type you want. If you're looking for a margin account, be sure that's what you get and not just a standard cash account form. Also, be sure to say if you intend to trade options or engage in short-selling.

As this book was being written, the discount brokerage industry was undergoing a major change in the way it signs up new clients. It used to be that discounters were required under the Know Your Client rule to do what was called a suitability check for each trade by a client. That is, check each trade against the investing objectives and risk tolerance that clients specified on their account applications. In April 2000, though, Canadian regulators announced that discounters (though not full-service brokers providing advice) would no longer have to perform these checks. This rule change was to alter the account application process somewhat. Most notably, there was an attempt to make it clear that clients are investing for themselves, with no supervision from the discounter. Clients now have to sign a form saying they understand that their discount broker does not provide advice or recommendations. As well, there will be a new emphasis on screening to ensure that applicants have enough investing knowledge and experience to run their own accounts.

Here's a rundown on the kinds of personal information required on an application form and the reasons why you have to supply these details.

- **Name and Legal Address:** It goes without saying that the discounter needs the name of the account holder. If the account is to be opened in the name of a club or corporation, the organization would place its name there. The legal address is required so that the broker has a physical address to which it can deliver documents. Although PO boxes and rural routes are the norm for country communities, a lot and concession number may be required

- **Social Insurance Number:** This is required by the Canada Customs and Revenue Agency for income tax reporting purposes. Brokers must report any interest earned by investors and keep the tax people abreast of RRSP details such as annual contributions and foreign content.

- **Citizenship:** Discount brokers are not permitted to open accounts for non-residents, although they can open accounts for non-citizens living in Canada. By comparison, some US discounters will open accounts for Canadians although this is technically prohibited under securities regulations. Typically they will have you sign a W8 form that says that you are subject to US withholding tax. Another reason for asking about citizenship relates to trading of "constrained shares." This refers to shares in companies that are restricted in foreign ownership, such as banks and telecommunications forms.

- **Employer, Occupation and Type of Business:** These questions have to do with policing of insider trading rules. Not only would the broker need to know who you are employed with and your position but they would also require spousal information in case the spouse was privy to insider information.

- **Family Information:** This is important for the same reason as the occupational details above.

- **Dependants:** This is related to the Know Your Client rule, but it can easily apply to the screening process as well. A person with no dependants may have a higher risk tolerance than someone with five kids under the age of 15.

- **Other Accounts with the Same Broker:** This helps brokers keep tabs on whether an individual might be trying to control the voting shares of a company. May also be used as a gauge for the broker to assess your experience.

- **Accounts with Other Brokers:** See above. Also indicates the experience level of the applicant. For instance, if you've already got two accounts at other brokers and have traded on margin with them, your new broker can be fairly confident that you possess the experience to manage a margin account with them as well.

- **Links with Exchange-Traded Companies:** Insider trading regulations require that clients disclose whether they are a senior officer or director of such a company and whether they control such a company by themselves or as a group.

- **Investment Knowledge:** This helps the broker determine how much risk you can absorb. If you want to trade options and other derivatives, you'll need to have a sophisticated level of knowledge. If you rate yourself as having little or no familiarity with investing, you may be limited to lower risk investments like mutual funds.

- **Investing Experience, Investing Knowledge, Investing Objectives, Risk Tolerance:** These are all questions that help the broker size up the ability of clients to trade on their own, without any supervision. Previously, these questions were asked to help brokers assess the suitability of client trades.

- **Income, Net Worth:** This has a bearing on the amount of risk a client is able to take. For example, someone with a six figure portfolio would generally be better able to absorb the risks associated with a risky options trade than would a student with no income.

- **Bank References:** This is for credit checks and for clients who want to have the money from their trades go directly into or from their bank accounts.

- **Signatures:** You will be required to sign the application in a number of places. The Investment Dealers Association of Canada now requires that a margin agreement (if applicable), options agreement (if applicable) and overall application agreement be signed. You may also be required to sign the RRSP section designating the beneficiary of the account's assets and as well the Policy 41/Shareholder communication section. That is not to mention other signatures for guarantees, power of attorney, debit and credit instructions. If it's a joint account, be prepared to provide both signatures everywhere. (Remember that RRSP accounts cannot be joint.)

- **Joint Accounts:** If you're setting up a joint account, you'll need to indicate whether the account is to be joint with rights of survivorship or tenants in common. Rights of survivorship means that if one of the account holders dies, the assets of the account will automatically transfer to the survivor. Tenants in common means that the assets of the deceased person goes to their estate. When you're setting up a tenants in common joint account, you'll have the opportunity to decide on how to split the assets of the account. Fifty-fifty is typical, but you can use any breakdown you want. Almost all couples who set up joint accounts choose the rights of survivorship option.

Details to Watch

If you're setting up an RRSP account, be sure to specify a beneficiary, be it your estate, your spouse or a surviving relative. If you want a margin account, the Investment Dealers Association of Canada requires a signed margin agreement. This is just boilerplate in which you acknowledge that you understand the terms of margin trading. There's a similar agreement to sign for options trading.

All application forms have either a separate page or special section to deal with something called National Policy Statement 41. Here's the background on this. Because the assets you hold with your broker are held in street form—in your broker's name and kept in safe custody for you—the company whose stock you purchased may not know that you are a shareholder. As a result, it's possible you won't receive the company's shareholder communications, including proxies, annual and quarterly audited financial statements and other information circulars.

That's where the National Policy Statement 41 section of the account application form comes in. In it, you'll be given two choices:

- Send all material related to annual or special meetings of security holders, including proxies and annual audited financial statements to me.

- I do not wish to receive the material relating to annual or special meetings of security holders or audited financial statements of the issuers whose securities I hold.

You'll then be asked:

You may disclose my name and security holdings to the issuer of the security or other sender of material required by law to be sent to securities holders in order that, at your option, material may be forwarded to me directly from the issuer or other sender of material: yes no

If you don't fill out the National Policy 41 material, you will not receive proxy related material regarding annual meetings and such. As well, the discounter has the option of disclosing your name, address and security holdings to the issuer of the securities held by you.

Other Forms

TRADING AUTHORITY (ALSO CALLED POWER OF ATTORNEY): This allows somebody else to trade your account for you and could be attractive if you're a novice at investing and want someone knowledgeable to handle your account. In some cases, people with zero investing experience might have their account application with a discounter rejected. If these people were to give a seasoned investor trading authority over the account, that might get the application accepted.

The trading authority form is a legal document that must be witnessed and signed by both the account holder and the person receiving account authority.

ACCOUNT TRANSFER: There are two different types of forms, one for registered accounts and one for non-registered accounts. In filling out these forms, be specific about which assets you want to transfer into your new account, and whether to transfer them in cash or in kind. Keep in mind that the transferring institution will charge a fee of $50 to $100 to process the transfer. Check to see if your new brokerage will pick up this cost. Charles Schwab Canada has in the past covered RRSP transfer costs of up to $100.

It's common to hear investors complain about the length of time it takes for accounts to be transferred from one broker to another. The Investment Dealers Association of Canada adopted a rule in September 1999 that says transfers involving member firms must be completed in 10 days. If your transfer is taking longer than that complain to the transferer first, then call the IDA and complain. The phone number is 416-364-6133.

In kind means the assets will be transferred as they exist in the account, which means stocks and mutual funds would transfer as they are. In cash means that the assets will be sold out and separate transaction commissions may apply. In cash is much faster.

GUARANTEE FORM: In the case of a student who is 18 or older, or a person who has no income to support their own investment activities, a broker may ask that the account be guaranteed by another individual.

Be sure to fill out all of the information required on the account application form. If you don't, you'll gum up the works by forcing the broker to follow up on the missing information at a later date. Even with your best efforts, chances are good that you'll still end up making a mistake or leaving out something important when you fill out the forms. By some estimates, more than half the applications submitted without assistance from a trained discount broker representative will require some follow-up.

The length of time needed to process an application and activate an account varies, but about two to five days is typical if you take your forms into a bank branch or an office of your broker that is open to the public. Add a few extra days if you mail your form. If you're lucky, someone from your new brokerage will call to tell you your account is active and give you your account number. If you haven't heard after several days, call them.

Rejections

Since discount brokers don't provide advice, they must ensure that clients have the ability to manage their accounts themselves. If a broker isn't satisfied that you have the investing experience or knowledge to manage your account, your application may be rejected. This doesn't happen often—usually only in one out of every 100 to 200 applications. More frequently, a broker might direct a new customer requesting a margin account into a cash account instead.

Step Four: On-line Set-Up

Once your account has been activated, you can immediately trade by telephone. If you want to go on-line, though, you'll need a password and user name. Some brokers, like Investor-Line, have streamlined the process by allowing you to specify your password on the account application, while E*Trade automatically assigns you a user name and a password. Most other brokers require you to call their electronic services office, where you'll be assigned a user name and a password.

When a password is assigned, the actual selection of the numbers or letters is done randomly by computer without human involvement. Brokerage staff just input the account information and the computer chooses the password. Assigned passwords are usually temporary. As soon as you sign into your broker's secure Web trading area, you'll be asked to choose a new one for yourself. Be warned—it can take your broker a day or two to get your password activated so you can trade on-line.

A few brokers require clients to have a trading password as well. You type this password in just before submitting an on-line order as a final way of verifying the person doing the trading is the account holder, or someone designated by him or her. When arranging your password and user name ask if a trading password is required. In some cases, E*Trade Canada for example, you just retype your regular password when asked for the trading password.

Step Five: Putting Cash in Your Account

It's important to make sure money is in your cash account before you start trading for the first time. After that, you'll usually have until the settlement date (generally three days for equities) of a trade to have the money in your cash account.

The two quickest ways to get money into your brokerage account for the first time are to send a cheque or, if your discounter is owned by the bank that you use, have your bank account debited. Bank-owned discounters make it easy to transfer money back and forth from a chequing account to a brokerage account, but you will have to sign a document authorizing the broker to do this. E*Trade Canada and Charles Schwab will electronically transfer money from most bank accounts as long as you supply them with void cheques.

If you are planning on sending a cheque, it's a good idea to have it certified or even to send a bank draft instead. Otherwise, you may have to wait five or six days while the cheque clears the bank. Don't send cash—brokers don't want it.

Ideally, setting up an account with a discount broker should be a relatively quick process. If the industry is in the midst of one of those periodic surges in client trading, however, you'll have to expect delays. RRSP season is one of those times. In the 1999/2000 RRSP season TD Waterhouse admitted to a two-week wait to get new self-directed RRSP accounts set-up and ready for on-line trading. Be patient. If one broker is extremely busy then they probably all are.

The more comfortable you get with using a discount broker, the more accounts you'll end up with. Maybe you'll start with a cash or RRSP account, then later add an RESP account. Eventually, you may decide to set up a margin account. Here are two pieces of advice in this regard. One, be sure to pick a broker that offers all the kinds of accounts you want, and that you can live with any fees that might be involved. Remember, some brokers charge annual administration fees for RRSP and RESP accounts (those that offer RESP accounts in the first place, that is). A second thing to remember is that when trading, be sure to double-check the account you specify. You don't want to end up buying that speculative penny tech stock for your RRSP when you meant to put it in your regular investing account.

4

Getting On-Line

With all the hype out there about on-line trading, you'd think there wasn't much more to it than just turning on your computer. But it's a little more complicated than that. For starters, let's take a look at your computer. Is it powerful enough to make your on-line experience an enjoyable one or is it going to struggle like an underpowered car going up a hill as you navigate your broker's Web site? Then there's the question of your Web browser, the software that allows you to call up a site and then move to another. If you haven't got the right version of your browser, you may be able to get into your broker's Web site but you likely won't be able to do any trading. What follows is a list of technical requirements for on-line trading. Read it and avoid the frustration of not being able to use your discount broker account the way it works best, on-line.

Your Computer

Central Processing Unit—You can surf the Internet with an old 486 computer, but it will be slow and you won't be able to have any other applications running at the same time. A Pentium computer running at 75 or 100 megahertz at least is better, while a Pentium II or Pentium III chip (or something equivalent) is ideal.

Memory—An absolute bare minimum is 16 megabytes of random access memory, though this will provide pitifully slow service. Thirty-two megs of RAM is much better, while 64 or 128 megs is ideal.

Operating System—All relatively recent versions of Windows and Mac systems are fine.

Modem—The minimum for adequate performance is 28.8 kilobits per second, but the 56K modems that are put in computers sold today are much better.

Your Browser

There are two main browser types in use, Netscape Navigator and Microsoft Internet Explorer, and it doesn't matter which you use as long as you have the right version. Some discount broker Web sites will work better if you have the 4.0 versions of either browser type or something newer. If you use an older version, you may find yourself getting bogged down with a lot of error messages.

To trade on-line, some discounters require that your browser be equipped with 128-bit encryption, also known as strong encryption. Problem is, most off-the-rack browsers tend to have less powerful 40-bit encryption. The difference is in the browser's ability to scramble the personal information you send over the Internet so that it can't be read by hackers. Fourty-bit encryption is exceedingly hard to crack without massive computing power, while 128-bit is virtually impossible. Many discounters allow their clients to use either encryption, but the preferred choice in the future will be the 128-bit version. Royal Bank Action Direct is one broker that currently supports both versions, but is encouraging clients to move to 128-bit encryption because it plans to eventually phase out support for the 40-bit technology.

If the standard is 128-bit encryption at your broker and you've got 40-bit, you'll still be able to prowl around the general

Web site but you won't be able to gain access to the secure Web trading area, even with a valid password and user identification. Fortunately, it's easy to upgrade a 40-bit browser to 128-bit encryption. If you use Netscape Navigator, head to www.netscape.com and find the page for browsers. The download is free, but you will have to register as a user. You can update Microsoft Internet Explorer for free as well at microsoft.com/windows/ie/default.htm (no www). A benefit of downloading strong encryption is that you get the latest version of your browser in the same package.

If you're not sure which level of encryption you have and your computer is equipped with Netscape Navigator, open your browser and click on the help buttom at the top. Next, click on "About Netscape" and look for a section marked RSA Encryption. A 128-bit browser will say: "This version supports U.S. security…," while a 40-bit browser will refer to international security. Internet Explorer will tell you which security level your browser works at when you log into a 128-bit site. Another method is to look at the bottom left corner of your browser. In Netscape, you'll know you have 128-bit encryption if you see a tiny padlock and then beside it, a tiny illustration of two pipe sections joined by a bizarre object looking a bit like the head of a bathroom plunger. If you have Internet Explorer, go to a secure Web site, put your mouse on the padlock symbol and look for a message saying "SSL Secured (40-bit)" or "SSL Secured (128-bit)".

Your Internet Service Provider (ISP)

Discount brokerage executives have been heard to put some of the blame for problems with their Web site on the Internet service providers of their clients, which is a fair comment but also a bit of a smokescreen for the broker's own technical inadequacies. The idea is that if you choose a second-rate ISP with equipment that frequently breaks down or can't handle heavy traffic, then your Web experience will suffer. Crummy ISPs will indeed cause problems, so don't just go for the cheapest rates. The main consideration is the ratio of lines to customers. Obviously, the more lines per customer the better.

Discount Broker Web Sites

If discounters have a face, it's their Web site. That's why most broker home pages (the Web page you get when you first call up a broker's Web site) are essentially a billboard designed to wow prospective new clients. Think of the actual contents of a broker's Web site as being like an on-line brochure filled with basic information about fees, investments available and other details. Most sites also offer stock market updates, stock quotes and a smattering of mutual fund and research tools. You won't find anything too elaborate in the way of toys, though. For those, you have to log into the secure portion of the Web site. Logging on for Web trading requires a user name and password chosen by you or the broker's electronic services people. Once you've logged in, you'll have access to the trading screen and a better variety of market information and research tools.

Most Web sites have a kind of table of contents somewhere on the home page. If you can't find what you're looking for, you can usually call up a detailed site map or do a search for all references to a keyword or phrase chosen by you.

After you've set up your account with a broker, take a few minutes to explore its Web site. Most brokers do only a so-so job of telling clients about all the services they offer, which means you may not know about a great research tool or market updates available on-line. Some brokers, such as Royal Bank Action Direct, also offer a list of links to other investing Web sites. If your broker allows you to customize a home page, take advantage. Usually, this is just a matter of selecting the market index and stock quotes you want to appear automatically when the page appears on screen. At Bank of Montreal Investorline for example, both clients and visitors to the Web site can set up a portfolio of stocks and monitor their gains and losses over time as well as track five separate lists of stocks for day-to-day movements and receive news bulletins for selected companies. E*trade Canada allows you to customize the home page you jump to after logging in with your user name and password. You can also set up your page to show updates and intraday charts on selected markets as well as news and quotes on stocks you're watching and links to your favourite investing Web sites.

Here's a complete list of discounter Web addresses and a quick review of how each site stacks up in terms of visual presentation and the ease with which you can find pertinent information if you're a prospective customer. Note that discounters often update their Web Sites, so some details mentioned here may have changed.

Bank of Montreal InvestorLine—www.investorline.com

Clean and easy to navigate, this is one Web site where they've anticipated the kinds of information users will be looking for and designed the site accordingly. Thus, information on products, services and commissions is very easy to find. A nice feature of this site is that both the regular Web site and the secure trading and account information site feature prominent stock market update charts. Another plus is that you can set up a customized personal page (you don't even have to be a client) with market summaries, news updates and 20-minute delayed quotes and charts on stocks you select. You can also load in a portfolio of stocks and track it over time.

Site Map: Yes

On-line Account Application: Yes

On-line Trading Demo: Yes

Charles Schwab Canada—www.schwabcanada.com

The Schwab Web site was redesigned in late 1999 and it looks a lot better than it did before. The home page isn't one of the more informative out there, but it does drive home the fact that Schwab is a "full-choice broker" as opposed to a conventional discounter (or a full-service broker). Overall, this is a well-organized site that lets you find information on things like commissions and fees with ease.

Site Map: Yes

On-line Account Application: Yes

On-line Trading Demo: Yes

CIBC Investor's Edge—www.investorsedge.cibc.com

We're betting the Investor's Edge Web site will be substantially improved in the time between the writing of this book and your reading it. How could it be otherwise? As it was, the site was one of the worst of any discount broker in Canada. Badly organized and downright ugly about sum it up. Compared to slick-looking sites like those from TD Waterhouse and E*Trade Canada, it looks especially hapless.

Site Map: No

On-line Account Application Forms: No

On-line Trading Demo: No

CT Securities—www.ctsecurities.com

A serviceable Web site that could be clearer and easier to use. Most of the information on the home page is contained under a few basic headings. If your query doesn't seem to fit into those or any of the other categories, there's no site map to fall back on. Nor is there any stock market information on the home page.

Site Map: No

On-line Account Application Forms: Yes

On-line Trading Demo: Yes

Disnat—www.disnat.com

A little rough-edged but usable. You have to root around some to find the information you're looking for, but it's all there. The look of the site is fuzzy and outdated. It would seem that Disnat, Canada's first discounter, hasn't updated its Web site in a while.

Site Map: No

On-line Account Application Forms: Yes

On-line Trading Demo: No

E*Trade Canada—www.canada.etrade.com

E*Trade is strictly an on-line brokerage, which means its Web site has a critical public relations function. This explains why the E*Trade Canada Web site is one of the better ones around. It looks crisp and clean and strikes a nice balance between hard information and PR puffery. E*Trade has made a play for the business of mutual fund investors and it shows on the Web site. There's a daily Top Five Fundschart of the previous day's big performers and a rudimentary search engine that lets you call up performance charts for all fund sectors.

Site Map: Yes

On-line Account Application Forms: Yes

On-line Trading Demo: Yes

HSBC InvestDirect—www.hsbcinvestdirect.com

This Web site means business. The log-in to the secure trading area is front and centre on the home page. If you're not a client, you can click onto an uninspiring home page that tells you all the basics about InvestDirect. Be sure to click on the FAQ (frequently asked questions) button, because that's where a lot of good information is.

Site Map: No

On-line Account Application Forms: Yes

On-line Trading Demo: Yes

National Bank Discount Brokerage—www.invesnet.com

Another serviceable job. Reasonably easy to navigate and find answers to typical questions a newcomer to the firm might have. There's no market data on the home page nor any toys of note.

Site Map: No

On-line Account Application Forms: Yes

On-line Trading Demo: Yes

Royal Bank Action Direct—www.actiondirect.com

This site isn't dazzlingly designed, but it is packed with information and simple to navigate. In fact, the Action Direct site is a model to others for making it easy for prospective clients to get the information they need. A bonus on the Action Direct site is the readily accessible and impressively complete list of links to investing Web sites. Just click on the research button on the home page.

Site Map: Yes

On-line Sign-up Forms: Yes

On-line Trading Demo: Yes

Scotia Discount Brokerage—www.sdbi.com

This Web site is an odd one. For one thing, it's among the plainest broker sites around. As well, there's a fair amount of information on it, but it's haphazardly arranged enough to make it hard to find basic details. If you want the commission schedule, for example, you have to click on the "top advantages" button and read down to the third entry, which is low commissions. Strangely, top advantage number one was an instant bonus on eligible back-end load mutual funds.

Site Map: Yes

On-line Sign-up Forms: Yes

On-line Trading Demo: No

Sun Life Securities—www.sunsecurities.com

Bright colours help bolster Sun Life's efforts to present a non-threatening place for novice investors. The problem is that there isn't as much information here as on other sites. For example, the site tells you what Sun Life's on-line commission rates are, but not its rates for broker-assisted trades done by telephone. If you're looking at Sun Life as a potential client, you may find you have to call to get answers to some of your questions as well as sign-up forms.

Site Map: Yes
On-line Sign-up Forms: No
On-line Trading Demo: Yes

TD Waterhouse—www.tdwaterhouse.ca

Crisp and friendly-looking, the appearance of this site is about what you'd expect from the leading discounter in the country. It's not the easiest site to navigate, though. For example, there's a site map but it's tricky to find. Also, there's no on-line demonstration of the Web Broker service, which is unusual considering that almost everyone else has one. On the other hand, this site is stuffed with information about the company.

Site Map: Yes
On-line Sign-up Forms: Yes
On-line Trading Demo: No

Complaints About On-line Trading

There's a simple answer to the question of why so many people complain about on-line trading. Though no broker promises it or even suggests it's possible, on-line trading implies instant gratification. You press the "submit" button and the trade should go right through. You call up a quote, the numbers should pop right up. You want to look at your account, the details should pour forth. This is more or less what happens in most instances, but there are still many times when on-line trading is just plain frustrating, even infuriating.

It's this gap between the promise of on-line trading and the sometimes disappointing reality that gets people so upset about discount brokers. Complain if you want to, but this is life with a discounter. On-line trading is not a perfected process. To expect it to work perfectly is naive.

The key factors influencing how fast a Web sites works are the number of people on the site at the same time, (called concurrence), and the quality and quantity of the broker's Internet hardware and software. But you can't just assume one broker will be faster than another because it has more servers in operation. If you're on the Internet at 3 a.m., every broker is going to seem like greased lightning. On a day when the market has gone crazy, even Ferrari-like Internet hardware is going to be choked by the volume of customers making sudden trading decisions or just pulling up quotes on the stocks in their portfolio. At E*Trade Canada, they say that volumes on busy days can be three times normal days.

When a flood of investors go on-line, the first sign of trouble will be that your broker's Web site responds to your mouse clicks more slowly. It may take a minute or so for the site to process your user name and password (if that doesn't sound like a long time, try sitting in front of your computer screen while your watch counts off 60 seconds), then even longer for your trade to be processed. In a worst case situation, you won't be able to log on, or if you can, you won't be able to get the Web site to process your order. One of the most frustrating things that can happen in on-line trading is when your screen freezes in the midst of submitting an order.

What's happening in these situations is not unlike what goes on when too many telephone calls overwhelm a switchboard. On a busy day, a broker will have all hands on deck but staff and computer systems can still get overwhelmed. Ultimately, a discounter may have to turn off the on-line trading pipeline to give it a chance to catch up on the order backlog.

Investor unhappiness with on-line trading has actually been a problem for awhile now. In January 1999, Arthur Levitt, chairman of the US Securities Exchange Commission, responded to grumbling on the part of investors by issuing a special statement about the need to have realistic expectations when using a discount broker. "Demand has grown so quickly that many firms are racing to keep pace with it," Mr. Levitt said in the statement. "In the meantime, you may have trouble getting on-line and/or receiving timely confirmation of trade executions. You should not always expect 'instantaneous' execution and reporting." The National Association of Securities Dealers (owners of Nasdaq) took a similar tack around the same time, telling members to inform investors that there may be times when high volumes of traffic will prevent them from gaining access to their accounts.

You'll notice that we've lumped all brokers together here as if they're all about the same in the quality of the on-line trading experience they provide to clients. Logically, there would have to be differences in Web site speed and the ability to keep up on busy days. But how do you tell who the fastest discounters are? You can't ask clients—if you check Internet investing message boards, all brokers seem to be ripped equally for their on-line service. One alternative is to look at an informal survey by Norman Rothery, a mutual fund analyst whose hobby is running one of the more interesting investing Web sites in Canada. Mr. Rothery looked at the speed issue by designing a computer program that downloaded the public home page of each discount broker hourly throughout the day. It's an inexact way to attack the problem because some broker home pages have more graphics than others, which will make them slower to load. As well, some sites will inevitably be slowed by the fact that they are being used by a larger client base than others. Still, Mr. Rothery's survey does at least give you a ballpark idea of how quickly a broker's Web site might work.

Figure 1: Rating Web Site Speed

Broker	Average Time to Load Home Page in Seconds
Bank of Montreal InvestorLine	5.37
Charles Schwab	2.75
CIBC Investor's Edge	2.97
CT Securities	3.13
Disnat	3.37
E*Trade Canada	4.83
HSBC InvestDirect	5.52
National Bank Discount Brokerage	2.87
Royal Bank Action Direct	3.96
Scotia Discount Brokerage	3.06
Sun Life Securities	3.46
TD Waterhouse	5.11

*(Source: Norman Rothery, Directions Web site: **www.ndir.com**).*
Check the site for the most up to date numbers.

Avoiding Trouble/Troubleshooting

If you want to avoid broker Web sites at their busiest then don't venture in during the daily rush between 9:30 a.m. to 10:30 a.m. That's the worst period of the day, worse even than the crush that happens between 3 p.m. to 4 p.m. as investors try to get their trades in before the markets end their regular trading sessions (several markets now have limited after-hours sessions each day).

If you submit a trade and you can't be sure if it was received by your broker then try the on-line order status screen. If that won't respond, try calling your broker's phone trading line to ask for an update. A representative will be able to tell right away whether the trade was processed and, if not, put it through for you. Make sure the commission for the transaction is priced at the on-line rate and not the more expensive phone rate.

If you can't enter a trade on-line because your broker's Web site is too overloaded then pick up the telephone. Don't expect quick action, though. If the on-line trading system is under a strain, the phones will be as well. On busy days, waits of 30 to 60 minutes or even longer aren't unheard of. If you're a customer of Royal Bank Action Direct or TD Waterhouse, consider using their direct dial-up systems. If you intend to use these services, you'll first have to load special software supplied by the broker onto your computer.

If you have persistant problems loading your broker's Web site check your Internet service provider. You'll know it's your ISP if all Web sites are slow to load and respond, not just your broker's.

If you want to get to your broker's trading screen as quickly as possible then bookmark the log-in page where you enter your user name and password. Going right to this page is much faster than downloading the broker's graphic-rich home page, then clicking on the "log in" button. You can also create bookmarks for other pages you use a lot such as a commission calculator or stock research tool.

Security

Your password and user name prevent anyone else from getting access to your account, provided you don't make the mistake of giving that information out to the wrong person. Some brokers take an additional security step of requiring you to enter a trading password when submitting each buy or sell order. The next line of defence is the encryption in your Web browser, which will prevent hackers from looking in on the personal information being relayed between you and your broker. This security doesn't protect e-mail correspondence, so never send personal account details to your broker by e-mail.

There's another aspect to security that you can look after yourself. When you visit a Web page, your browser will store it in its cache memory for future use. This includes pages in the secure Web trading area that might have your account details. Now, say you logged into your broker's trading area, checked your account, bought a stock, and then signed out and walked away from your computer. After that, somebody who came up to your computer would be able to view the Web pages with details on your account and the trade simply by pressing the "back" button on your browser a few times. To prevent this, exit your Web browser when you're finished using your broker's Web site. Alternatively, you can clear the cache. Here's how Bank of Montreal InvestorLine explains the process of clearing the cache:

If you are using Netscape Navigator 3.X:

1. From your browser menu select: Options.

2. From the Options drop-down menu select:
   Network Preferences.

3. From the Preferences window select: Cache.

4. From the Cache window select: Clear Memory Cache Now &
   Clear Disk Cache.

5. Then select the OK button at the bottom of the Cache window.

If you are using Netscape Communicator 4.X:

1. From your browser menu select: Edit.

2. From the Edit drop-down menu select: Preferences.

3. Under the Category list (on left side of the Preferences window), open the sub-menu for Advanced by clicking on the + symbol.

4. From the Advanced sub-menu, click on the word: Cache.

5. From the Cache window select: Clear Memory Cache and Clear Disk Cache.

6. Then select the OK button at the bottom of the Cache window.

If you are using Internet Explorer 4.X:

1. From your browser menu select: View.

2. From the View drop-down menu select: Internet Options.

3. From the Internet Options window select: General.

4. From the General window, look for the Temporary Internet Files section title near the middle of the window. Click on the Delete Files button.

5. A new window appears with the question "Delete all files in Temporary Internet Files Folder?" Click on OK.

6. Then select the OK button at the bottom of the Internet Options window.

As an added security measure in Microsoft Internet Explorer 4.X, you may decide to set your browser defaults as follows:

1. From your browser menu select: View.

2. From the View drop-down menu select: Internet Options.

3. From the Internet Options window select: Advanced.

4. From the Advanced scroll-down window, look for the Security section title. From this section, you may decide you prefer to select the following option: Do not save encrypted pages to disk.

5. Then click on OK at bottom of window.

In terms of log-in security, most discount brokers will freeze your account if you type in the wrong user name or password three times in a row. You'll have to telephone to free up your Web trading privileges.

If you forget your password: Call your broker and ask to speak to someone on the electronic services desk. You'll be asked to provide personal information, maybe your social insurance number, birthdate and so forth. You'll then be supplied with a new password.

Oddities

A few brokers do things differently than their peers in the on-line arena, usually to no great benefit to clients. A perfect example is Scotia Discount Brokerage's secure log-in system. You can't just call up the Scotia site, type in your password and user name and then start trading. Instead, you have to load special Scotia security software that creates a special icon on your computer desktop. Click on the icon and a secure browser window opens that asks for your password and user name, then takes you into the secure trading site. The drawback of this system is that you can't access Scotia's on-line trading service on just any computer. In fact, you can only download the security software on two computers, maybe your home computer and the one at work. (Where does that leave your notebook computer?) If you're already a Scotia client and you want to download the software for a second computer, the Web site to visit is www.scotia-bank.ca\IntFAQs.html port.

Royal Bank Action Direct and TD Waterhouse are among the few brokers to maintain both Web trading and a direct dial-up service whereby clients who have installed a special software package on their personal computers can use their modems to log directly into the broker's computer system. Direct dial-up systems appeared before the Internet came into wide use and have become redundant now that Web trading has taken off. The chief benefit for clients is that they can use the direct dial-up system as a backup in case the Web site is down.

In early 1999, a lot of discount brokers would have said that their clients split their trading fairly evenly between the Web and the telephone, but things are much different today. Now, two-thirds or more of trades at some of the larger discount brokers are done on-line and with good reason. When trading gets hot and heavy it's phone service that bogs down fastest. Web sites will get clogged as well and sometimes even become unavailable but they are still far more accessible than live representatives during busy times.

But the reasons for e-investing go beyond the simple ability to place a trade faster. Web sites are where most brokers add real value for clients. Research tools are there, market news is there and so is product news. Best of all, this information is available whenever you have a chance to go on-line. No broker will admit it, but clients who only use the phone are being relegated to second-class status.

5

Commissions and Fees

F act: Canadian discounter fees are generally far higher than in the United States. Fact: The differential for commissions may narrow, but not by much. TD Waterhouse, with its operations on both sides of the border, offers a good case study on how and why this situation exists. In the United States, the firm charges a flat $12 US for Internet trades up to 5,000 shares. In Canada, where parent Toronto-Dominion Bank is based, the best deal available is $29 Canadian for up to 1,000 shares. If you wanted to buy or sell 5,000 shares, the Canadian arm would charge you $150 based on a formula of three cents per share (with a cost greater than $2.01). If you're an active trader, this is a phenomenal difference. It's no wonder that more than a few Canadians have set up accounts with the American arm of TD Waterhouse to trade US stocks, rather than doing it through Waterhouse in Canada.

If you asked the firm why the price differential exists they'd probably start with economies of scale. TD Waterhouse has more than 2.1 million customers in the United States and more than 750,000 in Canada, or about one-third the US total. In addition, business costs like telecommunications are lower in the United

States. There have also been regulatory reasons why Canadian discounters have higher costs. Up until mid 2000, a discount broker in this country had to apply the Know Your Client rule to each trade while U.S. discounters did not. Every time an order came in via the Internet or telephone, someone at a Canadian discounter had to take it and scrutinize it against the client's stated investing goals and knowledge. This took time, and time, of course, costs money.

There's a third reason why US commissions are lower, and it has to do with the different marketplace south of the border. US investors tend to more aggressive. They keep higher balances in their accounts and buy on margin more often. With active customers like these, a broker can afford to keep commissions lower.

How much lower? Are you sure you really want to know? In the United States, you can place an on-line market order for as many as 5,000 shares for $8 at the deep discounter Ameritrade. Datek Online will let you place a market or limit order over the Internet for $9.99. On the other hand, there's a tier of US discounters with higher levels of service and higher commissions as well. For example, Charles Schwab charges $29.95 US for up to 1,000 shares traded on-line and three cents per share for orders involving more than 1,000 shares. That's pretty much what TD Waterhouse charges in Canada, but in US dollars. Now, that's pricey!

It also has to be pointed out that the Canadian discount market just isn't very competitive in the area of commissions. Of the 12 discounters examined in this book, all but two of them are in the $27 to $29 range for minimum stock trading commissions. InvestorLine has a $25 minimum for market orders, but charges $29 for the more commonly used limit order. The cheapest discount trade in Canada is Scotia Discount's $20 flat rate for trades of more than $2,000 in value. You'll almost always pay more than that because of the way its commission schedule works (see below for details). Scotia cut its commissions in the fall of 1998 in a bid to scoop up the business of cost-conscious equity investors. The response from the rest of the industry? Nada.

One reason to be optimistic about modest commission cuts in Canada is the rule change that eliminated the requirement for brokers to do a suitability check every time a client placed an order. Several discounters said in early 2000 that they would take a look at their commissions once the burden of having staff check each individual trade was eased.

In sharp contrast to stock commissions, the fees for mutual funds have fallen sharply over the past year or so. Discounters will still throw all kinds of little administrative fees at fund buyers, but the potentially costly upfront fees have mostly disappeared.

What follows is an explanation of the trends in stock, fund, bond and option commissions. Be sure to check with individual brokers for the latest pricing information.

Commissions for Stock Trades

This is where the money is made in the discount brokerage business, even though only one of every three trades is likely to be executed. For every on-line trade of under 1,000 shares that does get completed, the broker pockets anywhere from a minimum $20 at Scotia Discount Brokerage to a maximum of $29 at several brokers. Broker-assisted telephone trades bring in an average commission of about $40.

The differential between on-line and phone commissions is a considerable one, but it doesn't really reflect the cost differences between having clients enter trades themselves and paying brokers to take orders manually. In fact, trades placed through electronic avenues cost about 1/13th the cost of trades placed through a live agent. Still, the cost savings to investors are such that about two-thirds of trades are done on-line with the percentage rising all the time. Here's how commissions work for the different ways of trading.

On-line Trading

The usual practice is to charge a flat rate for trades of up to 1,000 shares. If you buy more than 1,000 shares, the commission is generally in the range of three cents a share for stocks trading at $5 and up. If you're buying a US issue, you usually just take the fee for Canadian stocks and convert it to US dollars.

Bank of Montreal InvestorLine

InvestorLine is one of two discounters in Canada to use the US pricing trick of differentiating between market orders and limit orders (Disnat is the other). Market orders, go for $25, while limit orders are $29. In either case, the commissions apply for purchases of up to 1,000 shares. Convert to US dollars for purchases of American stock. For orders of 1,000 shares or more:

Share Price	Commission Rate
0-$1	$0.005 per share
$1.01-$5	$0.02 per share
$5.01 and up	$0.03 per share
(minimum commission: $25 and $29)	

Charles Schwab Canada

Now here's a good example of how much you can save if you do it yourself on-line. Schwab offers both straight on-line trading and broker advisory services, and it prices accordingly. (It also offers phone trading with a live representative). Schwab differs from the rest of the pack by pricing its trades according to the value of the whole trade as opposed to share price. As you'll see, it makes for a more complex and potentially more expensive commission schedule, notably for smaller orders. Convert to US dollars for purchases of American stock.

Trade Value	On-line Commission Rate	Advisory Services Commission
$5,000 or less	0.75%	2%
$5,001–$10,000	0.50%	2%
$10,001–$40,000	0.25%	1%
$40,001–$100,000	.125%	.5%
> $100,000	.125%	.4%
(minimum commissions: $30 on-line; $100 advisory services)		

CIBC Investor's Edge

Take the following rates for broker-assisted Canadian equity orders and apply a 45-per-cent discount for stocks costing $5 or more and a 35-per-cent discount for stocks up to $4.99. Most trades of several hundred shares or less will come in at $28.

Share Price	Commission
$0.00 to $0.24	2.5%
$0.25 to $1.00	$35 + $0.005 / share
$1.01 to $2.00	$35 + $0.02 / share
$2.01 to $5.00	$35 + $0.03 / share
$5.05 to $10.00	$35 + $0.04 / share
$10.05 to $20.00	$35 + $0.05 / share
$20.05 and over	$35 + $0.06 / share
(minimum commission: $28)	

The same on-line discounts apply to this schedule for US equities (in US dollars):

Share Price	Commission
$0.00 to $0.24	3.0%
$0.25 to $1.00	$39 + $0.02 / share
$1.01 to $2.00	$39 + $0.03 / share
$2.01 to $5.00	$39 + $0.04 / share
$5 to $10.00	$39 + $0.05 / share
$10 to $20.00	$39 + $0.06 / share
$20 to $30.00	$39 + $0.07 / share
$30 and over	$39 + $0.08 / share
(minimum commission: $28)	

CT Securities

Very simple. The purchase of any shares in amounts of up to 1,000 costs $29. Convert to US dollars for purchases of American stock. The commissions for orders of more than 1,000 shares are as follows:

Share Price	Commission Rate
0.00 to $0.245	1.5% of trade
$0.25 to $1.00	$0.005 / share
$1.01 to $2.00	$0.02 / share
$2.01 +	$0.03 / share
(minimum commission: $29)	

Disnat

The original discounter in Canada keeps things clear. Buy up to 1,000 shares costing $2 or more and you pay $29. For more than 1,000 shares, the price is three cents a share. Purchases of shares costing less than $2 are always done at a commission of 1.5 per cent, with a $29 minimum. Convert to US dollars for purchases of American stocks.

E*Trade Canada

By and large, you'll pay $27 to buy up to 1,000 shares. Unfortunately, E*Trade makes you squint your way through the following chart to find this bit of news. Convert to US dollars for purchases of American stocks.

Stock Price	Share Volume	Transaction Fee
$1.00 and under	under 5,400 shares	$27.00
$1.00 and under	5,400 shares and over	$0.005 per share
$1.01 to $3.00	under 1,400 shares	$27.00
$1.01 to $3.00	1,400 shares and over	$0.02 per share
$3.01 and over	under 1,000 shares	$27.00
$3.01 and over	1,000 shares and over	$0.03 per share

(All transactions with principal value less than $3,500 will be charged a flat fee of $27.00)

HSBC InvestDirect

And now for something completely comprehensible. For shares costing $2 and more, pay $29 for up to 1,000 shares and three cents a share for more than 1,000. If your shares cost $1.99 or less each, pay 1.5 per cent, with a minimum charge of $29.

National Bank Discount Brokerage

Simple and attractively cheap as well. Any order for up to 1,000 shares costs $24.50. For more than 1,000 shares you pay 2.5 cents if the price is $2 or more and 1.4 per cent if the price is lower than $2.

Royal Bank Action Direct

A laudably straightforward commission schedule for its Net Action and PC Action, a direct dial-up service. For trades of up to 1,000 shares, the cost is $29. Convert to US dollars for purchases of American stock. For trades of more than 1,000 shares:

Share Price	Commission Rate
0-$0.245 cents per share	1.5% of trade
$0.025 to $1	$0.005 per share
$1 - $2	$0.02 per share
$2.01 and up	$0.03 per share

(minimum commission: $29)

Scotia Discount Brokerage

Scotia has some of the cheapest rates around for small purchases (large orders can get pricey), but also one of the least user-friendly commissions schedules. The idea is that on-line trades receive a 20 per cent discount off the following rate schedule:

Share Price	Commission
0-$1	$25 + half a cent per share
over $1 to $5	$25 + 2 cents per share
over $5 to $10	$25 + 3 cents per share
over $10 to $20	$25 + 4 cents per share
over $20 to $30	$25 + 5 cents per share
over $30	$25 + 6 cents per share

(flat rate commission of $20 or trades of less than $2,000)

Scotia has a separate schedule for US equities (in US dollars)

Share Price	Commission
0-$5	$35 + 4 cents per share
$5.125 to $10	$35 + 5 cents per share
$10.125 to $20	$35 + 6 cents per share
$20.125 to $30	$35 + 7 cents per share
$30.125	$35 + 8 cents per share

(minimum commission: $28)

Sun Life Securities

Canada's newest discounter takes the tried and true approach of charging a flat $29 for trades of up to 1,000 shares, providing the share price is $2.01 or higher. If the price is lower, then the commission for any number of shares is 1.5 per cent with a $29 minimum. If you buy more than 1,000 shares of a stock costing $2.01

or more, the charge is three cents per share. Convert to US dollars when purchasing American stock.

TD Waterhouse

Now you see where Sun Life got the idea for its pricing scheme—the two are identical! Convert to US dollars when purchasing American stock. The minimum commission is $29.

Commission Calculators

TD Waterhouse, Sun Life Securities and Royal Bank Action Direct are among the discounters that offer a commission calculator on their Web sites. Just type in the cost of the stock you're buying and the quantity and the calculator will tell you the cost. TD's is a little lame in that it only tells you the cost if bought on the phone. Action Direct's very nicely lays out the cost of the securities, the commission and the total transaction cost for buy and sells, with separate columns for on-line, automated phone and broker-assisted trades over the phone. A very useful feature.

Telephone Trading

The luxury of talking to a representative to place your order will generally set you back an extra $10 to $15 or so per order over unassisted on-line trading. Automated phone trading is all over the map. Some brokers regard it as being the same as on-line trading and price it identically. Others price it between live agent and on-line rates, which seems a bit greedy since neither on-line nor automated phone orders require a live representative to have contact with the client.

Another detail to be aware of is that the phone-on-line cost differential is even more pronounced when buying US equities. In many cases, a broker will convert its Canadian commissions into US dollars, then tack on an extra cent or two per share.

Here's a rundown on phone trading commissions. You'll notice that some brokers have a nice, clear system for pricing on-line trades but feel the need to produce long and dreary commission charts for phone trades.

Bank of Montreal InvestorLine

Speaking of those long and dreary charts... On the positive side, InvestorLine's $35 minimum phone rate is one of the lowest, and its automated phone trading system is priced at the same rate as Web trading.

Share Price	Commission Rate
$0.00 to $1.00	$35 + $0.005 / share*
$1.01 to $5.00	$35 + $0.02 / share
$5.01 to $10.00	$35 + $0.03 / share
$10.01 to $20.00	$35 + $0.04 / share
$20.01 to $30.00	$35 + $0.05 / share
$30.01 and over	$35 + $0.06 / share

*The maximum commission is 2.5% of the principal value of the transaction subject to a minimum commission of Cdn$35.

(maximum commissions for orders valued at $2,000 or less is $35)

Here's the InvestorLine rate card for US stocks (in US dollars):

Share Price	Commission Rate
$0.00 to $1.00	$35 + $0.02 / share
$1.01 to $2.00	$35 + $0.03 / share
$2.01 to $5.000	$35 + $0.04 / share
$5.125 to $10.00	$35 + $0.05 / share
$10.125 to $20.00	$35 + $0.06 / share
$20.125 to $30.00	$35 + $0.07 / share
$30.125 and over	$35 + $0.08 / share

(minimum commission: $35, which is also the maximum when the principal value is less than $2,000)

Charles Shwab Canada

Again, a little more expensive than the competition. Rates for its TeleBroker automated phone service are the same as those for on-line trading.

Trade Value	Commission Rate
$5,000 or less	1.5%
$5,001 - $10,000	1%
$10,001 - $40,000	0.5%
$40,001 - $100,000	0.25%
> $100,000	0.2%
(minimum commission: $50)	

CIBC Investor's Edge

See the rates printed in the earlier section, but forget about the 45-per-cent discount. There's a flat rate of $43 for trades of $2,000 and less and a minimum commission of $43. If you use the EdgeLine automated phone order system, you get the on-line commission discount.

CT Securities

A routine rate schedule. CT has no automated phone order system.

Share Price	Commission Rate
$0.00 to $0.24	2.5%
$0.25 to $1.00	$35 + $0.005 / share
$1.01 to $2.00	$35 + $0.02 / share
$2.01 to $5.00	$35 + $0.03 / share
$5.01 to $10.00	$35 + $0.04 / share
$10.01 and over	$35 + $0.05 / share
(flat rate: $39 for trades of $2,000 or less; minimum commission: $39).	

US commissions as follows (in US dollars)

Share Price	Commission Rate
$0.00 to $0.24	3.0%
$0.25 to $1.00	$35 + $0.02 / share
$1.01 to $2.00	$35 + $0.03 / share
$2.01 to $5.00	$35 + $0.04 / share
$5.01 to $10.00	$35 + $0.05 / share
$10.01 and over	$35 + $0.06 / share

(flat rate: $39 for trades of $2,000 or less; minimum commission: $39).

Disnat

Another typical rate schedule but with one interesting detail. If you place a market order, Disnat will reduce your commission by 10 per cent.

Share Price	Commission Rate
$0.00 to $0.50	2.0%
$0.51 to $1.00	$35 + $0.005 / share
$1.01 to $2.00	$35 + $0.02 / share
$2.01 to $5.00	$35 + $0.025 / share
$5.05 to $10.00	$35 + $0.035 / share
$10.05 to $20.00	$35 + $0.045 / share
$20.05 to $30.00	$35 + $0.055 / share
$30.05 and over	$35 + $0.065 / share

(flat rate: $42 for trades of $2,000 or less; minimum commission: $42)

US rates are as follows (in US dollars):

Share Price	Commission Rate
$0.00 to $0.24	3.0%
$0.25 to $1.00	$39 + $0.02 / share
$1.01 to $2.00	$39 + $0.03 / share
$2.01 to $5.00	$39 + $0.04 / share
$5.125 to $10.00	$39 + $0.05 / share
$10.125 to $20.00	$39 + $0.06 / share
$20.125 to $30.00	$39 + $0.07 / share
$30.125 and over	$39 + $0.08 / share

(flat rate: $42 for trades of $2,000 or less; minimum commission: $42)

E*Trade Canada

Broker-assisted trades cost $15 extra, which means a commission of $42 for most trades of up to 1,000 shares. The rates for using the automated Tele*master system are the same as for on-line trading.

HSBC InvestDirect

HSBC's rates for phone trades are very competitive. There is no automated phone system.

Share Price	Commission Rate
$0.00 to $0.24	2.5%
$0.25 to $1.00	$31 + $0.005 / share
$1.01 to $2.00	$31 + $0.02 / share
$2.01 to $5.00	$31 + $0.03 / share
$5.01 to $10.00	$31 + $0.04 / share
$10.01 to $20.00	$31 + $0.05 / share
$20.01 and over	$31 + $0.06 / share

(flat fee: $40 for trades of $2,000 or less; minimum commission: $40)

US commissions are as follows (in US dollars):

Share Price	Commission Rate
$0.00 to $0.245	3.0%
$0.25 to $1.00	$35 + $0.02 / share
$1.01 to $2.00	$35 + $0.03 / share
$2.01 to $5.00	$35 + $0.04 / share
$5.125 to $10.00	$35 + $0.05 / share
$10.125 to $20.00	$35 + $0.06 / share
$20.125 to $30.00	$35 + $0.07 / share
$30.125 and over	$35 + $0.08 / share

(flat fee: $40 for trades of $2,000 or less; minimum commission: $40)

National Bank Discount Brokerage

A cheaper minimum charge for broker-assisted trades than most of the competition.

Share Price	Commission Rate
$0.00 to $0.50	$35 + 2%
$0.51 to $1.00	$35 + $0.005 / share
$1.01 to $2.00	$35 + $0.02 / share
$2.01 to $5.00	$35 + $0.025 / share
$5.01 to $10.00	$35 + $0.03 / share
$10.01 to $20.00	$35 + $0.04 / share
$20.01 to $30.00	$35 + $0.05 / share
$30.01 and over	$35 + $0.06 / share

(flat fee: $35 for trades of less than $2,000; minimum commission: $35)

Here's the rates for buying US stocks (in US dollars):

Share Price	Commission Rate
$0.00 to $0.245	$35 + 2.5%
$0.25 to $1.00	$35 + $0.02 / share
$1.01 to $2.00	$35 + $0.03 / share
$2.01 to $5.00	$35 + $0.04 / share
$5.01 to $10.00	$35 + $0.05 / share
$10.01 to $20.00	$35 + $0.06 / share
$20.01 and over	$35 + $0.07 / share

(flat fee: $35 for trades of less than $2,000; minimum commission: $35)

Royal Bank Action Direct

Typical stuff for regular phone trading, although the US rates are marked up less than some others. Rates for TelAction, the automated phone service, are roughly a halfway point between online and live agent trading. With TelAction, you can buy up to 1,000 shares for $35. The rates for orders of more than 1,000 vary according to the share price. If you buy a stock worth $5 or more, the charge is four cents a share. Here are the regular phone rates.

Share Price	Commission Rate
$0.00 to $0.245	2.5%
$0.25 to $1.00	$35 + $0.005 / share
$1.01 to $2.00	$35 + $0.02 / share
$2.01 to $5.00	$35 + $0.03 / share
$5.01 to $10.00	$35 + $0.04 / share
$10.01 to $20.00	$35 + $0.05 / share
$20.01 and over	$35 + $0.06 / share

(flat rate: $40 for orders of $2,000 or less; minimum commission: $40.)

US rates are as follows (in US dollars):

Share Price	Commission Rate
$0.00 to $0.245	2.5%
$0.25 to $1.00	$35 + $0.02 / share
$1.01 to $2.00	$35 + $0.03 / share
$2.01 to $5.00	$35 + $0.04 / share
$5.01 to $10.00	$35 + $0.05 / share
$10.01 to $20.00	$35 + $0.06 / share
$20.01 and over	$35 + $0.07 / share

(flat rate: $40 for orders of $2,000 or less; minimum commission: $40.)

Scotia Discount Brokerage

See the rates listed earlier in this chapter, but drop the 20-per-cent discount. Overall, Scotia's phone rates are still cheap. The minimum commission for a trade with a live agent is $25 for Canadian stocks and US$35 for American stocks. Rates for the automated phone trading system are the same as for on-line orders.

Sun Life Securities

On the pricier side, especially for US stocks.

Share Price	Commission Rate
$0.00 to $0.24	2.5%
$0.25 to $1.00	$35 + $0.005 / share
$1.01 to $2.00	$35 + $0.02 / share
$2.01 to $5.00	$35 + $0.03 / share
$5.01 to $10.00	$35 + $0.04 / share
$10.01 to $20.00	$35 + $0.05 / share
$20.01 and over	$35 + $0.06 / share

(minimum commission: $43)

US rates are as follows (in US dollars):

Share Price	Commission Rate
$0.00 to $0.24	3%
$0.25 to $1.00	$39 + $0.02 / share
$1.01 to $2.00	$39 + $0.03 / share
$2.01 to $5.00	$39 + $0.04 / share
$5.125 to $10.00	$39 + $0.05 / share
$10.125 to $20.00	$39 + $0.06 / share
$20.125 to $30	$39 + $0.07 / share
$30.125 and over	$39 + $0.08 / share
(minimum commission: $43)	

TD Waterhouse

Also on the more expensive side for regular phone trading. TD takes much the same approach as Action Direct in pricing its automated phone service, called TeleMax, halfway between Web and live agent trading. Purchases of any amount of shares costing less than $2 brings a commission of 1.5 per cent with a $35 minimum. The flat fee for buying up to 1,000 shares costing $2 or more is $35; for more than 1,000 shares, TeleMax charges four cents a share. TD's Talk Broker voice recognition phone trading service is priced at $29.95 in most cases where less than 1,000 shares are bought. Here are the regular phone rates for Canadian stocks.

Share Price	Commission Rate
$0.00 to $0.24	2.5%
$0.25 to $1.00	$35 + $0.005 / share
$1.01 to $2.00	$35 + $0.02 / share
$2.01 to $5.00	$35 + $0.03 / share
$5.01 to $10.00	$35 + $0.04 / share
$10.01 to $20.00	$35 + $0.05 / share
$20.01 and over	$35 + $0.06 / share
(flat fee: $43 for orders of $2,000 or less; minimum commission: $43.)	

US rates are as follows (in US dollars):

Share Price	Commission Rate
$0.00 to $0.24	3%
$0.25 to $1.00	$39 + $0.02 / share
$1.01 to $2.00	$39 + $0.03 / share
$2.01 to $5.00	$39 + $0.04 / share
$5.125 to $10.00	$39 + $0.05 / share
$10.125 to $20.00	$39 + $0.06 / share
$20.125 to $30	$39 + $0.07 / share
$30.125 and over	$39 + $0.08 / share

(flat fee: $43 for orders of $2,000 or less; minimum commission: $43.)

WHO'S CHEAPEST?: Sorry to cop out here, but the answer is that it depends on the price of the shares and the quantity being bought. To give you some ideas about which brokers are cheapest in which circumstances, we have provided a few hypothetical stock purchases and the cost at all discount brokers. The numbers were crunched with the help of the commission calculator on the Directions Web site (**www.ndir.com**). For your information though, the cheapest you'll get a trade executed at any broker is Scotia Discount Brokerage Inc. at $20 for Internet trades with a value of less than $2,000. The most expensive is Charles Schwab at $30. The other minimum commissions are outlined in the chart below.

Figure 1: Absolute Minimum Fee

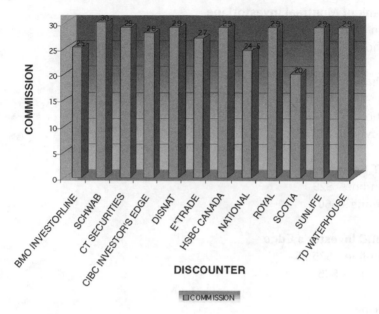

1. **Buying 500 shares of Loblaw at $35**

500 LOBLAW @ $35

	ON-LINE	PHONE	ADVISORY
BMO INVESTORLINE	25/29 (market/limit)	65	
SCHWAB	43.75	87.50	175
CT SECURITIES	29	60	
CIBC INVESTOR'S EDGE	35.75	65	
DISNAT	29	60.75/67.50 (market/limit)	
E*TRADE	27	42	
HSBC CANADA	29	61	
NATIONAL	24.5	65	
ROYAL	29	65	
SCOTIA	44	55	
SUNLIFE	29	65	
TD WATERHOUSE	29	65	

Bank of Montreal InvestorLine
On-line - $25 (market order)/ $29 (limit order)
Phone - $65

Charles Schwab
On-line - $43.75
Phone - $87.50
Advisory - $175

CT Securities
On-line - $29
Phone - $60

CIBC Investor's Edge
On-line - $35.75
Phone - $65

Disnat
On-line - $29
Phone - $60.75 (market order)/$67.50 (limit order)

E*Trade Canada
On-line - $27
Phone - $42

HSBC InvestDirect
On-line - $29
Phone - $61

National Bank Discount Brokerage
On-line - $24.50
Phone - $65

Royal Bank Action Direct
On-line - $29
Phone - $65

Scotia Discount Brokerage
On-line - $44
Phone - $55

Sun Life Securities
On-line - $29
Phone - $65

TD Waterhouse
On-line - $29
Phone - $65

Figure 2: 500 Loblaw @ $35

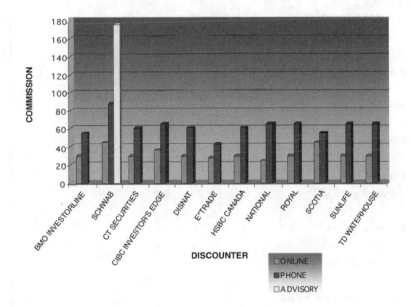

2. Buying 1,500 shares of Air Canada at $10

1500 AIR CANADA @$10

	ON-LINE	PHONE	ADVISORY
BMO INVESTORLINE	45	80	
SCHWAB	37.5	75	150
CT SECURITIES	45	110	
CIBC INVESTOR'S EDGE	52.25	95	
DISNAT	45	78.75/87.50 (market/limit)	
E*TRADE	45	60	
HSBC CANADA	45	91	
NATIONAL	37.5	80	
ROYAL	45	95	
SCOTIA	56	70	
SUNLIFE	45	95	
TD WATERHOUSE	45	95	

Bank of Montreal InvestorLine
On-line - $45
Phone - $80

Charles Schwab
On-line - $37.50
Phone - $75
Advisory - $150

CT Securities
On-line - $45
Phone - $110

CIBC Investor's Edge
On-line - $52.25
Phone - $95

Disnat
On-line - $45
Phone - $78.75 (market order)/$87.50 (limit order)

E*Trade Canada
On-line - $45
Phone - $60

HSBC InvestDirect
On-line - $45
Phone - $91

National Bank Discount Brokerage
On-line - $37.50
Phone - $80

Royal Bank Action Direct
On-line - $45
Phone - $95

Scotia Discount Brokerage
On-line - $56
Phone - $70

Sun Life Securities
On-line - $45
Phone - $95

TD Waterhouse
On-line - $45
Phone - $95

Figure 3: 1500 Air Canada @ $10

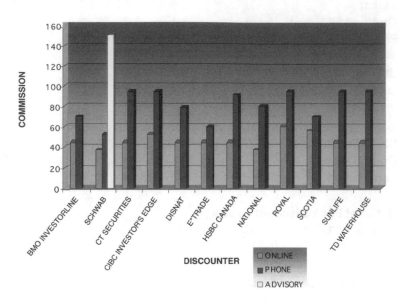

3. Buying 100 shares of Microsoft at US$92.87

100 MICROSOFT @US$92.87   (all figures in US dollars)

	ON-LINE	PHONE	ADVISORY
BMO INVESTORLINE	25/29	43	
	(market/limit)		
SCHWAB	46.43	92.87	185.74
CT SECURITIES	29	41	
CIBC INVESTOR'S EDGE	28	47	
DISNAT	29	42.30/47	
		(market/limit)	
E*TRADE	27	42	
HSBC CANADA	29	43	
NATIONAL	24.50	42	
ROYAL	29	42	
SCOTIA	34.40	43	
SUNLIFE	29	47	
TD WATERHOUSE	29	47	

Bank of Montreal InvestorLine
On-line - $25/$29   (all figures in US dollars)
Phone - $43

Charles Schwab
On-line - $46.43
Phone - $92.87
Advisory - $185.74

CT Securities
On-line - $29
Phone - $41

CIBC Investor's Edge
On-line - $28
Phone - $47

Disnat
On-line - $29
Phone - $42.30 (market order)/$47 (limit order)

E*Trade Canada
On-line - $27
Phone - $42

HSBC InvestDirect
On-line - $29
Phone - $43

National Bank Discount Brokerage
On-line - $24.50
Phone - $42

Royal Bank Action Direct
On-line - $29
Phone - $42

Scotia Discount Brokerage
On-line - $34.40
Phone - $43

Sun Life Securities
On-line - $29
Phone - $47

TD Waterhouse
On-line - $29
Phone - $47

Figure 4: 100 Microsoft @ US$92.87

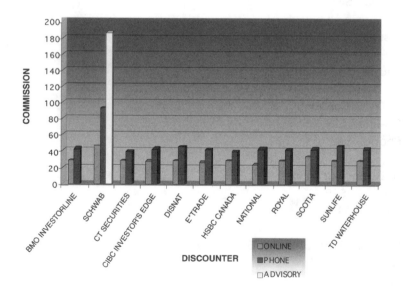

4. Buying 300 shares of Consolidated Aston Resources at $1.60

300 CONSOLIDATED ASTON RESOURCES @$1.60

	ON-LINE	PHONE	ADVISORY
BMO INVESTORLINE	25/29	35	
	(market/limit)		
SCHWAB	30	50	100
CT SECURITIES	29	39	
CIBC INVESTOR'S EDGE	28	43	
DISNAT	29	37.80/42	
		(market/limit)	
E*TRADE	27	42	
HSBC CANADA	29	40	
NATIONAL	24.50	35	
ROYAL	29	40	
SCOTIA	24.80	31	
SUNLIFE	29	43	
TD WATERHOUSE	29	43	

Bank of Montreal InvestorLine
On-line - $25/$29
Phone - $35

Charles Schwab
On-line - $30
Phone - $50
Advisory -$100

CT Securities
On-line - $29
Phone - $39

CIBC Investor's Edge
On-line - $28
Phone - $43

Disnat
On-line - $29
Phone - $37.80/$42

E*Trade Canada
On-line - $27
Phone - $42

HSBC InvestDirect
On-line - $29
Phone - $40

National Bank Discount Brokerage
On-line - $24.50
Phone - $35

Royal Bank Action Direct
On-line - $29
Phone - $40

Scotia Discount Brokerage
On-line - $24.80
Phone - $31

Sun Life Securities
On-line - $29
Phone - $43

TD Waterhouse
On-line - $29
Phone - $43

Figure 5: 300 Consolidated Aston Resources @ $1.60

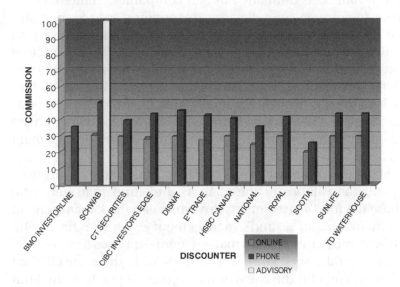

Commissions for Mutual Funds

Before looking at the fees and commissions that discounters apply to mutual funds, it's worth looking at the practices the fund industry itself uses. From the point of view of sales commissions, there are three different types of mutual funds. The first and simplest is no-load funds, which are sold without any commission but may require a modest account set-up fee. Front-end load funds charge an upfront commission that is expressed as a percentage of the amount invested, typically two to five per cent when you invest through an adviser. If a two-per-cent commission was applied to a $10,000 purchase, then $200 would be subtracted from the invested amount to leave $9,800. Back-end load funds, also called deferred sales charge (DSC) funds, levy a redemption fee if you cash out within six or seven years. Generally, the fee starts at six or seven per cent and gradually eases. In many cases, load funds are available in either front-end or back-end (DSC) versions.

All load fund companies pay trailer fees to brokers who sell their products, as do many no-load companies. Trailer fees are meant to compensate sellers for the ongoing service they provide fundholders and can amount as much as one per cent annually of the value of the funds purchased. There's another mutual fund cost and many believe it to be the most important one for investors to watch. It's the management fee and it's hidden because it is deducted annually from the fund's gross investment return. Those fund returns you see in newspaper charts and advertisements are always net returns, after management fees have been deducted.

Management fees go to cover trailer fees, overhead, advertising and the salaries of the analysts and fund managers who choose the fund's investments. Investors can track management fees by looking at a fund's management expense ratio (MER). The MER measures a fund's management expenses as a percentage of its total assets. The lower a fund's MER, the more efficient it is being run and the cheaper it is to own. If you take the MER and add it to the published gains of your fund, then you'll have a rough idea of your fund's gross return. Thus, MERs can be viewed as a rough gauge of how much return you're giving up so that your mutual fund company can pay its expenses and make a profit. A typical MER for a Canadian equity would be 2.3 per cent and for an index fund it would be below 1 per cent.

Discounter Commissions and Fees for Mutual Funds

In contrast to stocks, the cost of purchasing mutual funds through a discount brokerage account has fallen impressively. Although the purchase of front-end load funds through a full-service dealer can be negotiated, most discounters charged a customary 2 or 2.5 per cent upfront fee until recently.

Small funds-only brokers such as Altamira's Mutual Fund Direct set the trend for lower fund fees when they began several years ago to sell load funds without any commissions or fees, aside from an account set-up charge in some cases. One of the first of the larger discounters to push fund commissions lower was Canada Trust's CT Securities. In a move that was quickly copied, CT waived the commissions on transactions where the amount invested was greater than $2,500 and the client had

$15,000 or more in his or her account. Scotia Discount Brokerage waived front-end loads as well in Spring 1999, becoming the first of the bank-owned discounters to do so. Now, most discounters will offer front-end mutual fund purchases free of charge provided you place a minimum order that ranges between $1,000 and $2,500 and, in a few cases, have $15,000 or more in your account. Don't dismiss these commission reductions lightly. What they've done is effectively eliminate the distinction between no-load and front-load mutual funds while rendering the deferred sales charge fund obsolete.

Good riddance to those DSC funds, by the way. Once, they had some attraction in that they allowed you to get into a load fund without having to pay an upfront commission. Now that discounters have largely done away with those commissions, there's no reason to buy a DSC fund and thus put yourself in the position of possibly having to pay a redemption fee if you decide to bail out.

Despite the lack of appeal of DSC funds, some brokers have tried to build up their business in this category with cash-back offers. For a minimum purchase of $2,500 some brokers will give you an additional 2.5 to 3 per cent of your capital in the form of extra fund units. If you bought $10,000 of a DSC fund at Scotia Discount Brokerage, for example, you'd get $300 worth of fund units tacked on. Of course, all redemption fees apply. In fact, they apply to the extra $300 as well.

Discounters have done well in their treatment of load funds, but they need work on no-load funds. In fact, it's safe to say that investors are more likely to encounter an unpleasant surprise fee or commission when buying no-load funds than they are with load funds.

The problem is that some no-load mutual fund companies—Phillips, Hager & North and Bissett would be examples—don't pay trailer fees. That means there's no way for a discounter selling these funds to make money on a continuing basis. If you're buying one of these funds, expect to pay a 1 or 2 per cent upfront commission. Fund companies that pay no trailer fees can often be spotted through their ultra-low MERs. If you're interested in one of these funds, be sure to check with your broker to find out if there are any fees involved.

Another cost sometimes associated with no-load funds is the account set-up fee. If a no-load company charges such a fee, the discounter will usually pass it on. That's the case with Altamira Investment Management, which charges $40 to set up a new account. Most discounters also charge a redemption fee when you cash out of a no-load or front-load fund. If you like to hold your cash in a money market fund, be warned that some brokers levy their redemption charges on these funds just as they do on others.

If you're looking for the closest thing to fee-free fund investing, consider the in-house funds offered by all the bank-owned discounters. As a rule, discounters charge no fees for buying, switching or redeeming these funds. Bank funds are as a rule mediocre performers, but each family has at least one or two winners you may want to consider, while some have more. If you're looking for a money market fund, definitely go with the in-house fund.

So far, all we've looked at are commissions and fees associated with buying and selling funds. Many brokers also have switching charges for moving your money between funds in the same family. The list below rounds up all fund costs at each broker.

Bank of Montreal InvestorLine

No commissions on front-load funds and a 2.5 per cent rebate on DSC funds that rises to 3 per cent if you buy on-line. The minimum initial purchase is $1,000. InvestorLine has no switch fees, but it does levy a $40 charge to redeem both front- and no-load funds.

Schwab Canada

Early in 2000, Schwab joined the majority of discounters in eliminating commissions on front-load funds, although in Schwab's case this only applies to on-line purchases. Here are Schwab's full range of fees for front-load funds.

On-line	Broker-Assisted Over the Phone	Advisory
$0	$39	2% capped at $299 (minimum: $39)

There are no redemption charges for any front-end load funds at Schwab but there is a $39 charge for redeeming no-load funds over the phone or through an advisor. (No-load fund redemptions are free on-line). Schwab charges no switch fees, other than a $50 charge for advisory clients who want to switch a rear-end load mutual fund.

CIBC Investor's Edge

Commissions on the purchase of front-end funds were waived in early 2000. If you switch or redeem such a fund within 90 days of purchase, though, a sales commission will be applied upon redemption. The schedule is:

Value of trade	Commission	Internet charge
$1,000 - $5,000	2.5%	2.25%
$5,001 - $24,999	2.0%	1.75%
$25,000 and over	1.0%	.75%

Note also that effective July 1, 2000, a $30 fee will apply to switches and redemption orders on front-load funds. There are no redemption charges for front-load funds, but no-load fund redemptions cost $40 (except for money market funds). There are no fees to buy no-load or DSC funds.

CT Securities

You can choose from over 600 mutual funds and pay zero commission fees under CT's OneStop program, but there's a minimum account size of $15,000 and a minimum investment of $2,500 per fund. Zero really means zero here—there are no purchase, redemption or switch fees.

If you're not using OneStop, then you'll pay a 1.5-per-cent commission on front-load funds bought over the phone and a 1.25-per-cent commission for on-line fund orders. For no-load funds, there's a $39 redemption fee.

Disnat

More than 600 funds are offered with no front-load fee as long as you buy a minimum of $1,000 worth. For other front-load funds, there is a 2 per cent commission on purchases of up to $25,000 and a 1 per cent charge on amounts above that. A $45 redemption fee applies to zero cost front-load funds, and to no-load funds. Disnat has no switch fees.

E*Trade Canada

Couldn't be simpler or more investor-friendly. There are no fees or commissions to buy, sell or switch funds, although a 1 per cent fee (minimum $38.88) is applied on the sale of funds held for less than 90 days.

HSBC InvestDirect

Simple and generally cheap. There are no commissions on front- and no-load funds but a $40 redemption fee on both. There's also a $40 fee to switch money between funds in the same family.

National Bank Discount Brokerage

Another member of the minority of discounters who charge a front-end load on mutual funds. If you're buying up to $24,999, the commission is 1.75 per cent on phone orders and 1.225 per cent for on-line orders. For trades valued at $25,000 or more, the commissions are 1 per cent and .7 per cent respectively. There are no redemption or switch fees for front-end load funds. For no-load funds, there's a $40 redemption fee for phone customers and a $28 fee for those investing on-line.

Royal Bank Action Direct

There are no commissions on front-load funds provided you have assets of at least $15,000 in your account and place an order for $1,000 or more. Otherwise, commissions for funds bought on-line are 2.25 per cent for purchases of up to $4,999, 1.75 per cent for purchases of $5,000 to $24,999 and .75 per cent for $25,000 and over. Add an extra .25 of a percentage point for broker-assisted orders. As well, there's a $40 redemption fee for no-load funds.

Scotia Discount Brokerage

There are no front-load commissions on 400 different funds as long as you buy a minimum of $2,500. Otherwise, if you buy up to $25,000 worth you pay a 2 per cent commission with a minimum of $50. For more than $25,000, you pay a 1 per cent commission. Buy on-line and you get a 25 per cent discount, with a minimum of $20. Scotia is big on little fees as well. There's a $15 redemption charge for front- and no-load funds and for DSC funds as well, which is a bit of a money grab when you consider you'll quite likely face a penalty fee from the fund company as well in this situation. Two other sneaky fees: A $25 administrative charge when you buy no-load funds and a switch charge of up to 2 per cent for front-load and DSC funds.

Sun Life Securities

There are no fees for buying front-load, no-load and rear-load funds. A $45 redemption fee applies to no-load and front-load funds, but it's discounted by 25 per cent if you trade on-line. No fees for switching inside the same fund family.

TD Waterhouse

There is no charge to buy most front-load funds, as long as your order is worth $1,000 or more. Unlike some other discounters there's no minimum account size required to get this benefit. Note the $45 redemption fee for front- and no-load funds.

THE 90-DAY CHARGE

Some brokers discourage investors from jumping in and out of funds by slapping a charge on those who sell within 90 days of purchase.

Commissions for Bonds

Bonds appear to be sold commission-free, but they're not. The commission is just included in the price you're quoted for a bond, effectively hiding it from view. Whatever price a broker is offering you for a bond, it paid a little less.

If you used a full-service broker, you might be able to negotiate a lower price for the bond you want to buy and thus you'll get a higher yield (yield and prices move in opposite directions). Brokers will do this for their good clients. Ironically, you won't get a preferential rate from a discounter unless you're placing a very large order of $50,000 to $100,000.

Commissions for Options

Bank of Montreal InvestorLine

The following rates for telephone option trades are discounted by 20 per cent for on-line orders. If the principal value of the trade is $2,000 or less, the maximum commission is Cdn$35 or US$45.

Option Price	Commission per Contract
$0.00 - $1.00	$29 + $1.00
$1.01 - $2.00	$29 + $1.50
$2.01 - $3.00	$29 + $2.00
$3.01 - $4.00	$29 + $2.50
$4.01 - $5.00	$29 + $3.00
$5.01 plus	$29 + $3.50

Charles Schwab

Schwab's commission schedule is again graduated according to the amount of assistance you use.

Canadian and US Options*	Electronic Services	Broker-Assisted	Advisory Services
All prices	$30 + $1.50/contract	$40 + $1.50/contract	$100 + $1.50/contract
Minimum	$31.50	$41.50	$101.50
*US commissions in US dollars			

CT Securities

Here are the rates for option trades done by telephone. For on-line trades, discount these rates by 20 per cent.

Contract Value	Commission per Order*
$0 - $2	$35 + $1.50/contract
$2.01 - $3	$35 + $2.00/contract
$3.01 - $4	$35 + $2.50/contract
$4.01 - $5	$35 + $3.00/contract
$5.01 and over	$35 + $3.50/contract
*US options in US dollars; minimum commission: $39	

CIBC Investor's Edge

Options - Purchase and Sale	
Price	Commissions
$0 - $2	$35 + $1.50 per contract
$2.01 - $3	$35 + $2.00 per contract
$3.01 - $4	$35 + $2.50 per contract
$4.01 - $5	$35 + $3.00 per contract
$5.01 and over	$35 + $3.50 per contract

Disnat

The same charges apply regardless of whether the trade is made on-line or by phone. The minimum commission is $30, whether its in Canadian or US funds. The charge for orders valued at less than $2,000 is $30.

Price	Canadian commission per contract	U.S* commission per contract
$0.00 to $2.00	$25.00 + $1.50	$30.00 + $1.25
$2.01 to $3.00	$25.00 + $2.00	$30.00 + $1.75
$3.01 to $4.00	$25.00 + $2.50	$30.00 + $2.25
$4.01 to $5.00	$25.00 + $3.00	$30.00 + $2.75
$5.05 & over	$25.00 + $3.50	$30.00 + $3.25
*US dollars		

E*Trade Canada

Take the following on-line rates and add $15 for a broker-assisted transaction. Convert to US dollars for purchase of US options.

Contract Price	Contract Volume	Transaction Fee
$2.00 and under	Under 25 contracts	$38.88
$2.00 and under	25 contracts and over	$1.50 per contract
$2.01 to $4.00	Under 20 contracts	$38.88
$2.01 to $4.00	20 contracts and over	$2.00 per contract
$4.01 and over	Under 13 contracts	$38.88
$4.01 and over	13 contracts and over	$3.00 per contract

HSBC InvestDirect

Discount the following phone commissions by 20 per cent for on-line orders. Convert to US dollars for purchase of US options.

Option Value	Commission
$0- $1	$35 + $1.00 per contract
$1- $2	$35 + $1.50 per contract
$2.01- $3	$35 + $2.00 per contract
$3.01- $4	$35 + $2.50 per contract
$4.01- $5	$35 + $3.00 per contract
$5.01-and over	$35 + $3.50 per contract

National Bank Discount Brokerage

The minimum commissions are $21 for on-line orders and $30 for broker-assisted orders. Convert to US dollars for purchase of American options.

Option price	Commission with a representative	On-line Commission (minus 30 per cent)
$0 - $1.00	$30.00 + $1.00 per contract	$21.00 + $0.70 per contract
$1.01 - $2.00	$30.00 + $1.50 per contract	$21.00 + $1.05 per contract
$2.01 - $3.00	$30.00 + $2.00 per contract	$21.00 + $1.40 per contract
$3.01 - $4.00	$30.00 + $2.50 per contract	$21.00 + $1.75 per contract
$4.01 and over	$30.00 + $3.00 per contract	$21.00 + $2.10 per contract

Royal Bank Action Direct

Take 20 per cent off these phone commission rates for on-line orders and 10 per cent for orders made on Action Direct's automated phone system. The minimum commission is $40 and a $40 flat rate applies to orders of less than $2,000. Convert to US dollars for purchase of US options.

Option Price	Commission Rate
$0.00 - $2.00	$35 + $1.00/contract
$2.01 - $3.00	$35 + $2.00/contract
$3.01 - $4.00	$35 + $2.50/contract
$4.01 - $5.00	$35 + $3.00/contract
$5.01 and over	$35 + $3.50/contract

Scotia Discount Brokerage

The following rates are for broker-assisted Canadian option orders. US option trades have a US$35 base rate plus the applicable contract commissions. Scotia does not yet offer on-line options trading.

Option Value	Commission
$1 or less	$25 + $1.00 on 1st 10 Contracts + $0.50 on each additional
$1.01 - $2.00	$25 + $1.25 on 1st 10 Contracts + $0.75 on each additional
$2.01 - $3.00	$25 + $1.50 on 1st 10 Contracts + $1.00 on each additional
$3.01 - $4.00	$25 + $1.75 on 1st 10 Contracts + $1.25 on each additional
$4.01 - $5.0	$25 + $2.00 on 1st 10 Contracts + $1.50 on each additional
$5.01 and up	$25 + $2.50 on 1st 10 Contracts + $1.75 on each additional

Sun Life Securities

On-line trades take a 20 per cent discount off these rates. US orders are in US dollars.

Option Value	Commission
$ 0 - $2	$ 35 + $ 1.50/contract
$ 2.01- $3	$ 35 + $ 2.00/contract
$ 3.01- $4	$ 35 + $ 2.50/contract
$ 4.01- $5	$ 35 + $ 3.00/contract
$ 5.01 over	$ 35 + $ 3.50/contract

TD Waterhouse

Take 20 per cent off these telephone commission rates for on-line orders and 10 per cent off for trades made on TD's automated phone line. Convert to US dollars for purchase of American options.

Option Value	Commission
$0-$2	$35 + $1.50 per contract
$2.01-$3	$35 + $2.00 per contract
$3.01-$4	$35 + $2.50 per contract
$4.01-$5	$35 + $3.00 per contract
$5.01 and over	$35 + $3.50 per contract

*

As you see from the comparisons provided in this chapter, it's impossible to say definitively which broker is cheapest on commissions. The best piece of advice when comparing commissions is to first get a clear idea of what kind of trading you'll be doing. If you plan to buy funds mostly and sprinkle in a few stocks, then it will be more important for your broker to have no fund commissions than low stock commissions. If you plan to momentum trade, where you buy and sell frequently, then cheap stock commissions will be very important. Don't make price your only consideration, though. A few bucks saved on a trade will mean nothing if every other aspect of a broker's service is unsatisfactory.

We've tried to include the very latest information on commissions, but some of the numbers will inevitably change as time goes by. For this reason, be sure to check all commissions and fees mentioned here against what's listed on broker Web sites.

6

Buying Stocks Through a Discounter

If you want to know how to trade stocks through a discount broker, don't ask a discounter. More and more brokers are explaining how to place an order on their Web sites, but all you'll find is bare-bones information that really doesn't tell the whole story. Overall, there seems to be an unspoken rule that if you have to ask basic questions about trading then you really shouldn't be using a discount broker.

Trading stocks isn't rocket science, but there are some techniques and strategies that can save you money and help you avoid the disappointment of not having your order filled. Here then, is a primer on how to trade stocks with a discount broker. Mutual funds, bonds and options are covered in subsequent chapters, but we've devoted the most space to stocks because that's what the vast majority of discount broker clients are interested in.

The purpose of this book is to give you the tools needed to trade effectively through a discount broker and also to make use of the investing resources available on the World Wide Web. If you feel you need to do some more learning before you're comfortable investing yourself, check out any bookstore's investing section or the Web sites listed at the end of this chapter as well as Chapter One.

Getting Ready to Place a Stock Trade

There are eight steps to getting started in buying stocks through a discount broker.

Step One: Be Sure of Which Shares You're Buying

Let's assume you've done your research and picked a stock you want to buy. Your next step is to do a little preparatory work that will get you ready to trade. First, find out exactly which share issue it is that you want to buy. Many companies have several shares listed on an exchange and it can cause some confusion if you're not certain which one it is that you want to buy. In some cases, a company might have several common and preferred share issues trading on an exchange. For example, the Bank of Montreal has six issues trading on the Toronto Stock Exchange— five of them preferred and one common.

Another distinction between a company's shares might be that some have voting rights while others do not. Voting shares are sometimes denoted by an *sv* in newspaper stock tables, which stands for subordinated voting shares. Some companies, Bombardier would be an example, have class A and class B common shares. If you want to know which of the two classes is more actively traded, check the trading volumes and go with the most active of the two.

DID YOU KNOW?

Clients of discount brokers made 11 million trades in 1999, compared with 7.5 million in 1998.

(source: Investor Economics)

Step Two: Get the Stock Symbol

Once you're sure which shares you want, get the stock symbol. If you're trading on-line, this is easily done by heading to your broker's Web site and then using the quote look-up button. If you're trading over the phone, you can look up the symbol in the newspaper or on the Internet.

The representative who takes your telephone order probably knows all the most popular stock symbols by heart, but she doesn't necessarily remember those for shares traded on the Canadian Venture Exchange or Nasdaq. If you, for example, placed an order to buy 100 shares of Blond Bear Holdings (BB:X) and the trader wasn't familiar with the stock, she would have to look the symbol up in order to place the trade. Doing this is relatively easy and fast, but there is always some risk you might end up buying the wrong stock.

Stocks on most exchanges have a two- or three-letter symbol (in rare cases, such as Inco's N, it's a one-letter symbol) under which the company trades. Canadian companies keep the same symbol, no matter which domestic exchange they trade on, but they will often have a different symbol when listed on a US exchange. Corel Corp. is COR on the TSE and CORL on Nasdaq; Canadian Imperial Bank of Commerce is CM on the Toronto Stock Exchange but BCM in New York; Nortel Networks is NT in both Toronto and New York. Note that Nasdaq and Canadian over-the-counter stocks have four-letter symbols.

Step Three: Decide How Much You Want to Buy or Sell

Most stock trades are in board lots, which generally means 100 shares. On the TSE, if the share price is less than $1, then 500 shares constitutes a board lot; if the price is under 10 cents, then a board lot is 1,000 shares. Some exchanges may have different rules for board lots. Anything that isn't a board lot is called an odd lot. If you're trading odd lots of shares, there may be times when you have to pay a slight premium on buy orders and accept a little less on sell orders. This will mainly happen with illiquid stocks (those that either trade infrequently or in small volumes) or in thinly traded markets.

The number of shares you can afford should only play a relatively small role in your decision to purchase a security. If you had wanted to acquire 100 shares of JDS Uniphase two years ago (when it was JDS Fitel) you might have found the cost of buying a board lot too high and decided to wait until the price dropped into a range where you could afford the 100 shares. Unfortunately, you would have missed out on a huge appreciation in the price of JDS stock.

Step Four: Get a Quote

A well-designed on-line trading screen allows you to call up a quote while entering in the particulars of your order. In these cases, the quote will pop up in a second window in your browser or within the order screen itself. Later we'll examine how to use this quote information in making your trade. Right now, though, it's important to understand how these order screen quotes differ from the run-of-the-mill quotes available on just about every investing Web site out there. Order screen quotes are generally in real time, which means they are based on the latest trading action on the stock exchange in question. Elsewhere on the Web, the quotes are usually delayed 15 or 20 minutes. In a fast-moving market, a 20-minute-old quote ago is about as good as one from the week before.

DID YOU KNOW?

If you want to keep track of what the major North American stock markets are doing through the day, bookmark the Web site of RBC Dominion Securities, the full-service brokerage. The DS site at **www.rbcds.com** refreshes itself every five minutes, which means it provides market updates in five-minute intervals.

Unfortunately, on-line quotes are not as detailed as you can get from a broker when placing a trade over the telephone. Either source will give you basics like the bid, ask, last trade and volume, plus whether the stock is up or down and by how much. On the telephone, though, you can also ask about the sizing and depth of the market (we'll explain these terms in a moment).

Of course, the most detailed quote in the world is useless unless you know how to read and interpret it. Here's a sample of a highly detailed quote for BCE Inc., Canada's most widely held company, complete with explanations of all the jargon. The quote as relayed by a broker might sound something like: BCE bidding $120.95, asking $121.05; last traded at $121.05; sizing 200 by 65. It's up 35 cents today on a volume of 1,250,000 shares. It's traded between $120.70 and $121.05 today with a 52 week range of $65 to $121.05.

Here's what all that means:

Bid: The bid is the highest price someone is willing to pay for a stock, specifically a board lot with no restrictions on the order. Our quote shows that $120.95 is the most investors are willing to pay for BCE shares at the moment.

Ask: The ask is the lowest price that a seller is willing to accept for a board lot of a stock. Here, sellers have indicated they'll take no less than $121.05. When the bid and ask are the same, a trade is executed and the next highest bid and next lowest ask take their place.

Last Trade: The price at which the most recent trade was executed. The most recent trade of BCE shares came at the asked price of $121.05.

Sizing: This refers to the number of board lots on each side of the market. In the above example, the first number in the sizing refers to the bid side, so there were 200 board lots or 20,000 shares worth of buy orders for BCE at $120.95. The second number refers to the asked side, so there were 65 board lots or 6,500 shares placed as sell orders at $121.05.

Change: The increase or decrease in the share price from the previous session's closing value. BCE is up 35 cents on the day.

Volume: This refers to the number of shares traded that day. In our example, 1,250,000 shares had traded by the time the quote was given. Volume is a key indicator of investor interest. High volume may mean institutional involvement or that news has been released. Low volume could indicate illiquidity, which suggests it may be difficult to sell a position in the stock.

Open: This is the price at which the first trade of the day is executed.

Previous Close: This is the price at which the stock last traded on the previous trading day. This is also discernable from the change in the stock's price as indicated above in "Change".

Day Hi/Day Low: This trading range gives the investor an idea of which direction the stock is moving in. In our example BCE stock has risen and is now trading at its high on the day. A trader can tell you if the last trade was higher or lower than the last by providing an up-tick or down-tick indicator.

52-Week Range: This range tells the upper and lower limit of where the stock has been in the previous 12 months. It's no indication of where the stock is headed.

Depth: Most of the quote details listed so far come under the heading of a Level One quote. For depth, you'll require a Level Two quote. The complication here is that Level Two quotes are generally only available through representatives and not through broker Web quotes, even the detailed real-time quotes provided on stock order-entry screens.

The depth of the market takes the sizing a step further and discloses how many board lots are posted behind the bid and the ask prices. If the bid price is $120.95 and the sizing is 200, depth would show how many board lots were posted to buy at the next level of one nickel or dime less.

How our BCE quote examples might look if you got it on-line						
Bid	Ask	Last	Open	DayHigh	Day Low	Change
$120.96	$121.05	$121.04	$120.70	$121.05	$120.70	+.35

Volume	52-week high	52-week low	Current Yield	P/E Ratio
1250000	$121.05	$65	1.73	22.47

Note that the on-line quote is less detailed than the oral quote in some ways, but it also gives you additional information on a stock's dividend yield and price to earnings ratio.

Step Five: Decide What Kind of an Order to Place

It's not unheard of for novice discount broker clients to say "What do you mean?" when asked by a trader what type of order they would like to place. These investors just assume a buy is a buy and sell is a sell. On the contrary, there are a variety of different types of orders, each of which will accomplish different things.

Here's a rundown on the various kinds of orders and when to use them. Please note that you have to specify a particular type of order when trading both on-line and through a representative on the phone. There is no "default order" that kicks in if you don't state which type of order you want.

Market Order

When you buy at the market, you're telling the trader to buy a specific number of shares of the stock at the best price available at the moment. The upside is that you'll get near instantaneous execution. If you're trading by phone, you'll likely get a confirmation of the trade before you hang up. For on-line trades, confirmation should come up in a matter of a few minutes, although it can take as long as an hour during exceptionally busy periods.

Market trades are risky, though, particularly when trading is heavy and/or volatile. When your order is executed, there's no guarantee it's going to be at the price that was in effect when you placed the order. If you're buying in a fast-rising market, you could end up paying a lot more than you anticipated. Conversely, you could get a lot less for the shares you're selling than you expected in a volatile or falling market.

Sometimes when a large market order is placed, some of the shares might be filled at different prices. If an order was placed to buy 10,000 shares but there were only 3,000 available at the prevailing asking price, the remaining 7,000 could be filled at the next price level or higher. If you used a market order, your transaction will be executed at whatever the market price is. You should be particularly wary of placing a market order after trading hours are over. By the time your order is executed the next morning, the price for the stock may be much different than its closing price the day before.

WHEN TO USE A MARKET ORDER:

1) When for some reason you must have your trade executed immediately.

2) When you want to own a high-flying stock and are willing to accept the risk that the price may have surged by the time your order is processed. This is known as momentum trading.

3) When you're buying a relatively tame stock for a long-term hold and you're not too concerned about the price moving a lot.

Limit Order

This is the most common type of order and the one you should use for most trades. When you place a limit order, you're essentially setting a maximum that you're willing to pay or a minimum that you're willing to accept.

"Buy me 100 shares of Air Canada, symbol AC, on the TSE at $10.00" is a limit order in which the trader has been told to buy the stock for the best price up to and including $10.00 per share, but no more. A sell order works the same way. "Sell 100 shares of my Hudson's Bay, symbol HBC (the symbol is not absolutely necessary on sells because the trader can see what's in the account), at $25.00" means the trader's instructions are to get the best price possible to a minimum of $25. If you're trading online, you can specify limit versus market order and then type in your limit price.

NOTE ABOUT PRICE DISCRETION

While a limit order by definition includes a maximum buying price or minimum selling price, some brokers will allow you to give them what's called price discretion on the order. In other words, you can give the trader the discretion to pay a little more or accept less in order to get your limit trade executed. There are no guidelines for how much price discretion to give your broker—it could be as little as a few cents or a dollar or two, depending on how expensive the shares are. Ask about price discretion when placing a phone trade. If you're trading on-line, look for a price discretion box on the on-line order screen.

The appeal of a limit order is that it protects you against buying a stock when the price has surged ahead of what you want to pay or can afford. A limit order can also ensure a floor price for shares that you want to sell. The downside of limit orders is that there's no guarantee your order will be filled. Or, you may only get part of your order filled—a partial fill in trading lingo.

WHEN TO USE A LIMIT ORDER:

1) When you think the price of a stock may jump, and you don't want to get caught in the updraft. A limit buy order essentially says you're willing to pay up to a set amount for the stock and no more.

2) When you want to sell a stock at a price that allows you to lock in a set profit.

3) When you want to strategically buy/sell a stock at a predetermined price. Say Air Canada stock has risen in each of the previous three days to $10 and even though it will likely rise over the coming months, you expect that in the short term it will fall. You would then place a limit order to buy the stock at say, $9.65. You would also likely want the order to remain open for a few days so that you don't have to keep replacing it.

So far we have looked at two very simple order types—market orders and limit orders. Generally, these orders can be executed very easily through the Toronto Stock Exchange's computerized trading system. If you place one of the next group of orders, though, you'll be placing restrictions on your order.

The result is that your order will have a lower priority and be harder to execute. Bottom line, you'll have less chance of making the trade you want.

DID YOU KNOW?

When making a buy order at the market's opening, market orders and limit orders *above* the opening price will have priority over limit orders that match the opening price.

Orders With Restrictions

Placing an order with restrictions is like giving your broker an extra set of instructions on how you want your trade handled. You might, for example, specify that you want all the shares you requested to buy or none at all, or you might say you're willing to accept a minimum number of shares. The problem with restricted orders is that they're more complicated to execute because they must go into what's called the special terms market. Let's look at how these different order types are handled on the Toronto Stock Exchange.

When a routine order for a TSE-listed stock is received, it's executed once it hits the exchange floor by a system called the TOREX. Orders with restrictions are more complicated because a TSE specialist must get involved to ensure the trade is executed in a timely way. The end result is that the order does not get executed with the same speed that an unrestricted order would. In busy markets, orders with restrictions may very well not get executed at all. Bottom line, a market order would be confirmed by your trader while you wait on the phone, a limit order would be executed slightly less quickly and orders with restrictions still less quickly.

There are five or six different kinds of order restrictions, but most discounters only offer a few. "All-or-none" and "Minimum" orders are most common.

All-or-None Order

This means you want to buy all of the shares in the order and, if they all cannot be filled at the same time, then don't execute the order. If you want to buy 500 shares of a company that is somewhat thinly traded and you place an AON restriction on the trade, it's possible the trade will not be filled even if the purchase order was placed at the asking price. Some brokers recommend you trade in board lots if you use an all-or-none order.

Minimum Order

This is similar to an all-or-none except you're willing to accept a minimum of say, 500 shares out of on order to buy 1,000. It's always possible you'll get more than your minimum and if you do, it will be in increments of one board lot (100 shares).

Stop-Loss Order

In Canada, a stop-loss order is an order to sell a security when the price of a board lot trades at a price set by you, the so-called stop price. A stop-loss order effectively becomes a market order when your price limit is reached.

There are no guarantees as to what price a market order will get filled at, which is why we strongly recommend that you consider placing a stop-loss with a limit. In this case, you would specify the stop price and also a limit price with the idea that the order would be executed somewhere between the two but not below the limit.

Suppose you own a stock that has had a nice run-up in the past few weeks, rising as high as $10 from $5.50. You think that in the short-term, the stock price may come under pressure, so you place a stop-loss order for $9.00, good for a week, with the aim of locking in a $3.50 capital gain. If the stock comes under selling pressure and it trades at $9.00 then your stop-loss would be triggered. Trouble is, with the stock falling, you might find that your shares are sold at a price of $8 or less and not $9. For this reason, you might want to place a stop limit at $8.75. This tells the trading floor that the lowest price you're willing to accept is $8.75 and if the stock trades below that not to sell. Obviously, you won't want to use a stop limit if you absolutely must dump a stock.

You cannot place a sell order and a stop-loss order on the same stock at the same time. This prevents you from selling the same stock twice. Stop loss orders on orders less than 100 shares are invalid and would be rejected by the floor.

WHEN TO USE A STOP-LOSS ORDER

People will sometimes use stop-loss orders when they're away on vacation and can't monitor their portfolios.

For US-listed stocks, a stop-loss is slightly different in that it is triggered when the price of a board lot is bidding at your indicated price.

Stop-Buy Order

This is similar to a stop-loss order, except the point is to buy a stock when the price of a board lot trades at a limit set by you. A stop-buy order also becomes a market order when your price point is reached.

WHEN TO USE A STOP-BUY ORDER:

1) To reduce possible losses when a stock you're short selling starts to rise. Essentially, short selling means you would borrow shares from your broker (or your broker's client)—shares that you do not own— and you would sell them with the intention of buying them back at a better, lower price. If the stock that you've shorted rises, the risk inherent here is that you'd have to buy the stock back at some astronomically high value. That's where the stop-buy order comes in. It allows you to buy the stock back to protect yourself against any further losses.

2) If you want to participate in the upward momentum of a stock but don't necessarily want to buy it now. You'd place a stop-buy order at a price that to you would indicate that the share value was about to spike. One benefit here is that if the stock ends up falling, you won't participate in the decline.

Step Six: Interpret the Quote

An actively traded stock will usually have a small spread. That is, the difference between the bid price and asked price will generally be within a nickel to 50 cents (depending on the value of the stock). If you want to get a buy order done quickly, you might put in a limit order at the asked price. This is virtually the same as a market order, although you're safe if the asked price spikes upward before your order is processed. The same holds true if you're selling—you put your order in at the bid price.

The spread on an illiquid stock might be substantial. Since buyers and sellers are far apart, you could try submitting a limit buy order at a price that is halfway between the bid and the asked. The idea is that there's not much demand for the shares, so the seller might bite at your offer.

> If you're placing a restricted order or trading in odd lots, your best chance of success is to put your trade in at the asked price if you're buying and the bid price if you're selling.

If you're placing a large order, pay close attention to sizing and depth (remember, you'll probably have to call a representative find get depth numbers). You want to know how many shares are available at the bid/asked price, and, if there's not enough to fill your order, how many shares are available at the next best price.

Watch the volume for signs the stock you're buying is riding a wave of upward or downward momentum. If volume is well ahead of its average daily level, then it's quite likely the stock is experiencing a significant price change. This would have important implications for investors placing market orders.

Step Seven: Decide How Long the Order Will be Good For

You'll either place a day order, which expires at the end of the day, or a good-through order (also called a good-till-cancelled or GTC order), which expires at the end of a date specified by you. A day order is cancelled at the end of the day if it is not filled at all or in part. Say a limit order was placed and only 200 shares

were filled of a total order for 500. The remaining 300 shares
would be cancelled, just as the whole order would be if no shares
were bought. Market orders are an exception here since they are
usually executed immediately.

Most brokers will allow a maximum of 30 days for a good-
through order. Remember that if a large-size order is left open for
more than a day, you open yourself to the possibility of paying
multiple commissions. On an order for 3,000 shares, you might
find your broker has filled 1,000 on the first day and 2,000 on the
second. That would mean two commissions. If you used a day
order and it was filled in two instalments in the same day, then
only one commission would be charged.

In researching a stock, it may be that you found a price at
which it represents a good buy. There's no reason you can't place
an order at that price and make it good for a set period of time.
Maybe you like Inco at $15. Instead of placing a trade for Inco
immediately at the prevailing price of $17.25, you would place
an order to buy 500 shares at $15 "good for a month."

A NOTE ABOUT TRADING HOURS

Trading hours end at 4 p.m., the standard closing time for North American stock markets. These days, though, it's possible to trade into the
early evening on several stock exchanges including the TSE and Nasdaq.

On Nasdaq, you can place and revise orders during an extended session that runs from 4 p.m. to 6:30 p.m. Think of this extra session as a
separate trading period. Orders placed during regular hours don't apply
after 4 p.m. If you want to place an order during the later session, you
have to wait until after 4 p.m. and also specifically mention that the trade
is for the extended session. Only limit orders and day orders are allowed.

The TSE's last sale trading session allows investors to trade from 4:05
p.m. to 5 p.m. All transactions must be done at the last sale price during
regular trading hours. If you have an open order with no restrictions that
you placed during regular trading hours, then it will automatically apply
for the later session provided the price is the same as or better than the
last sale price. Only board lot trades with no restrictions are eligible. If
you want to get an order in before the standard 4 p.m. close, don't wait
any later than 3:45 p.m. Of course, that applies to a normal trading day.
On busy days, you'll have to get your order in even sooner. Note that the
Canadian Venture Exchange closes at 4:30 pm.

Step Eight: Decide How to Settle the Trade

Here are your choices of how to pay for stocks you're buying. You can use cash in the trading account, sell money market fund holdings or Treasury bills, use available margin or debit the money from a bank account. You may also use the proceeds from a confirmed sale in the account, provided they're enough to cover the cost of the shares you're buying. If there are assets in the account that are sufficient to cover the value of the trade, you may also be able to write a cheque. If you deal with a bank-owned discounter, drop your cheque off at a branch of the bank and ask that it be sent to the broker through internal mail. Don't mail it.

Trade settlements are three days for equities, which means you have to have the money in your broker's hands on the third business day after the day of your trade. If you place a trade on Monday, trade settlement is on Thursday. The credit department of the discounter may want you to pay for your trade earlier, or if you've just signed up with a broker or haven't traded in a long time, they may ask that there be funds in the account at the time the trade is placed. In those cases, the trade will be settled in one day, which means the money will be debited in a day's time. Mutual funds settle in three days as well, although money market funds settle the next business day. Other money market instruments settle the same day. Bonds of three years and less in term settle in two days, longer-term bonds settle in three days.

Avoid settling a trade late. If this happens, you will have to pay interest on the amount you owe and your account could be flagged as delinquent. This means you could be asked to pay up front for your next trade. Remember that if you don't settle your debt, your broker can sell the securities in your account to cover what you owe.

A NOTE ABOUT FREE RIDING

This is a term that means buying a stock with the intention of selling it the next day and never planning to actually pay for the shares purchased. Brokers will flag your account if you do this with the possible result being that you'll have to pay up front for trades.

Figure 1: E*Trade Canada's stock order entry screen
Here's how you'd buy 200 BCE Emergis shares.

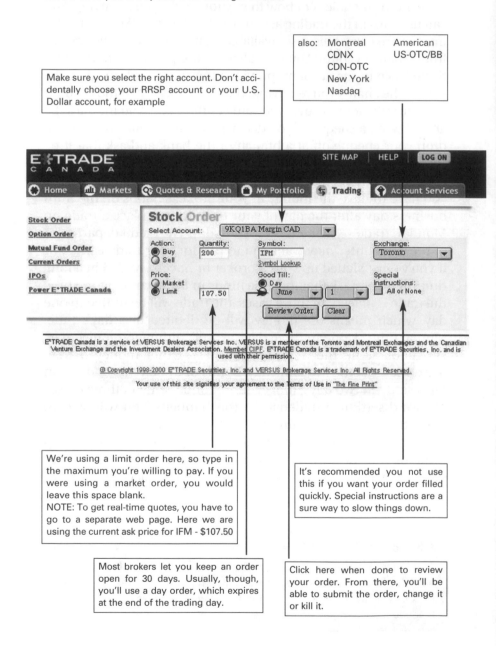

also: Montreal American
CDNX US-OTC/BB
CDN-OTC
New York
Nasdaq

Make sure you select the right account. Don't accidentally choose your RRSP account or your U.S. Dollar account, for example

E*TRADE
C A N A D A

SITE MAP | HELP | LOG ON

Home   Markets   Quotes & Research   My Portfolio   Trading   Account Services

Stock Order
Option Order
Mutual Fund Order
Current Orders
IPOs
Power E*TRADE Canada

Stock Order

Select Account: 9KQ1BA Margin CAD

Action: Quantity: Symbol: Exchange:
○ Buy   200   IFM   Toronto
○ Sell   Symbol Lookup

Price: Good Till: Special
○ Market   ○ Day   Instructions:
● Limit   107.50   June   1   ☐ All or None

Review Order   Clear

E*TRADE Canada is a service of VERSUS Brokerage Services Inc. VERSUS is a member of the Toronto and Montreal Exchanges and the Canadian Venture Exchange and the Investment Dealers Association. Member CIPF. E*TRADE Canada is a trademark of E*TRADE Securities, Inc. and is used with their permission.

@ Copyright 1998-2000 E*TRADE Securities, Inc. and VERSUS Brokerage Services Inc. All Rights Reserved.

Your use of this site signifies your agreement to the Terms of Use in "The Fine Print"

We're using a limit order here, so type in the maximum you're willing to pay. If you were using a market order, you would leave this space blank.
NOTE: To get real-time quotes, you have to go to a separate web page. Here we are using the current ask price for IFM - $107.50

It's recommended you not use this if you want your order filled quickly. Special instructions are a sure way to slow things down.

Most brokers let you keep an order open for 30 days. Usually, though, you'll use a day order, which expires at the end of the trading day.

Click here when done to review your order. From there, you'll be able to submit the order, change it or kill it.

Figure 2: E*Trade Canada's order review screen

Here's what you'd see after placing the order for 200 BCE Emergis shares. Keep your eye on the ask price here. If it's up or down from your earlier quote, you can still adjust your order to reflect this.

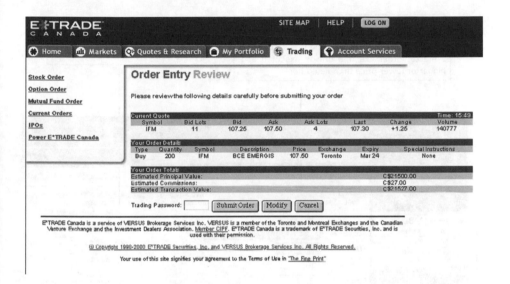

Figure 3: E*Trade Canada's order confirmation screen

This is what you'd see after submitting the BCE Emergis order.

Figure 4: Royal Bank Action Direct's Stock order entry screen

Here's how you'd buy 100 Mobile Computing Corp. shares.

This is a real-time quote, which means it reflects the latest trading information. Things can change quickly, though, so don't be surprised if a market order like this one is executed at a higher or lower price than listed here.

We're using a market order here, which means we're willing to pay the going market price.

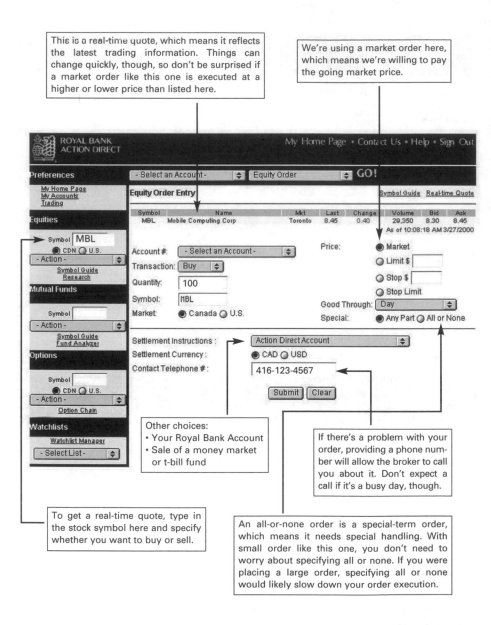

Other choices:
• Your Royal Bank Account
• Sale of a money market or t-bill fund

If there's a problem with your order, providing a phone number will allow the broker to call you about it. Don't expect a call if it's a busy day, though.

To get a real-time quote, type in the stock symbol here and specify whether you want to buy or sell.

An all-or-none order is a special-term order, which means it needs special handling. With small order like this one, you don't need to worry about specifying all or none. If you were placing a large order, specifying all or none would likely slow down your order execution.

Figure 5: Royal Bank Action Direct's order review screen

This is your last chance to change the order before it goes to a trader.

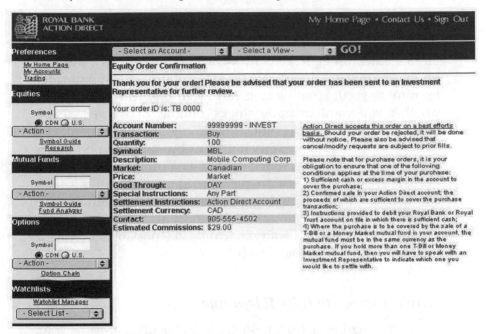

Figure 6: Royal Bank Action Direct's order confirmation screen

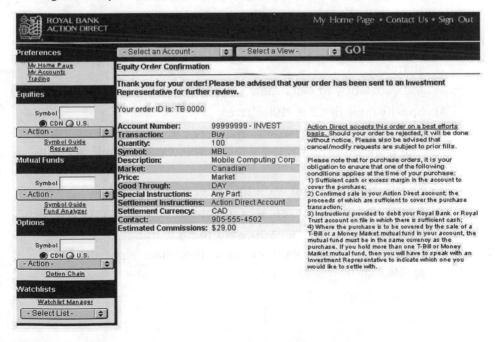

Now You're Ready to Trade

Here's How to Do It On-line

It's easier to show you than explain it, so we've included some on-line stock order screens in this chapter. Generally, though, on-line trading requires that you go to your broker's Web site and log into the secure trading area. Most Web sites will then ask you whether you want to trade stocks, options or mutual funds. When the order screen comes up, simply fill in the blanks by either typing in the necessary details or by using the pull-down menus. Don't worry too much about filling things in wrong. For one thing, your order will be presented back to you for a final check before it's submitted to a trader. Second, discount broker Web sites are designed to send a warning note up on your screen if you do anything procedurally wrong, like possibly entering a limit order without a specified price.

Here's How to Do it by Telephone

1) After reaching a trader on their 1-800 line, provide your name, account number and type of account. You may also have to verify who you are, possibly through a password or by providing a birthdate.

2) Give the name of the security and any specifics, e.g., class A shares.

3) Indicate a buy or sell order.

4) Specify quantity, e.g., 100 shares.

5) Specify whether you want a market or limit order and, if the latter, specify which special terms you want to apply, e.g, all or none.

6) Specify how long you want the order to remain open.

7) Mention if the order replaces or cancels an earlier order.

8) Specify which currency you want to trade in.

9) Indicate how you want to settle the trade, e.g., pay from assets in broker account.

The conversation to buy a stock might sound like this

Client:	Hi, I'd like to place a trade.
Trader:	What's the account number?
Client:	22-222-2222B
Trader:	What stock did you want to buy?
Client:	Bombardier Class B
Trader:	How many shares?
Client:	200 shares.
Trader:	At what price?
Client:	$22.50
Trader:	Any restrictions?
Client:	Yes, all-or-none, please.
Trader:	And how long is the order good for?
Client:	Just till the end of the week. The 18th.
Trader:	And how did you want to pay for that?

Client:	Margin, the rest of the cash is in my bank account.
Trader:	OK. Let me repeat that. That's 200 shares Bombardier B at twenty-two and a half, all-or-none, good till the end of the week and we're using available margin, debiting your bank account for the difference. Is that correct?
Client:	Yes. Thank You.

While this conversation is going on, the trader will review the account for such things as:

– the client's profile for risk tolerance
– securities in the account
– existing open orders that might affect this latest trade
– cash availability
– foreign content (for RRSPs)
– trading authority
– settlement instructions
– margin authorization

Depending on the security you're buying you may also be asked in what currency you would like the trade to settle in.

If the trade was to replace or change an order previously placed, the trader would advise that the transaction is subject to "prior fill." This simply means that you can't kill or change an order that has been executed. Keep in mind that an order may have been filled but not reported back to the client.

Now Review the Trade

As you can see from the sample phone trade above, a broker will double-check all the details of your order. With Web trading, you have the opportunity to see your order as opposed to hearing it.

The order entry process on-line always ends with the client clicking on a button that says something like "review" or "validate order." What follows is a verification screen that lists all terms of the order and, sometimes, a tally of the estimated cost of the trade with commission broken out separately. If you want to kill the order, you can do it at this point, or you can change your order. Once you're happy with the way the order looks, just press the "submit order" button. At this point a few brokers will ask you to type in a special trading password to complete the process as a final security check.

After receiving your submitted order, your broker will send back a standard confirmation page that may give a bare-bones summary of your transaction or a breakdown complete with an estimated total cost based on your limit price or the bid and asked price for the security at the time of ordering, plus commission. You'll also get a confirmation number, which you'll need if there's a problem with the trade and you have to discuss it with your broker. If you have a printer handy, it's not a bad idea to print a copy of your order confirmation page so you can have the trade particulars handy.

Remember, the cost of a market order that you see on the order confirmation or verification screens is just a guess based on the latest trading developments. The price of the stock you're buying or selling could fall or rise by the time the order is executed, changing the overall cost significantly.

A NOTE ABOUT LATE FILLS

The Canadian Venture Exchange has been known (more so than the senior stock exchanges) for late fills. A late fill is when a trade has been executed but not confirmed to the client's broker. Thus the broker would not have a record of the transaction, and the client would be in jeopardy of changing a trade (or cancelling it) based on the assumption that the order was not filled.

Here's How to Trade Using an Automated Phone Service

Most brokers allow you to both get quotes and trade over an automated phone system that you use by pressing various combinations of buttons on the phone keypad. Annoyingly, many brokers expect you to know how to use the system before you call in. The main trick you have to learn is how to spell out stock symbols using the phone buttons. If you want a quote for a stock with a symbol that starts with the letter N, for example, you first press the keypad number 6. You then have to press the number 2, which represents the position of the letter N on the key. You have to follow this two-step procedure for every letter in the stock symbol.

If it sounds complicated, it's not. However, it is tricky in that you have to pay close attention to each button you press. This isn't something you want to be doing on your car phone while trying to merge onto the highway at rush hour. If you plan to use your broker's automated phone line, be sure to ask for one of those pocket-size brochures that spells out exactly which keys you press to do whatever transaction that you want to do. It's a real time saver because you can type in the right sequence of numbers without having to wait for the taped prompts.

**Buying Nortel Networks Shares on the Automated Phone Line
at Bank of Montreal InvestorLine**

Step 1:   Call the 1-800 or local number in your area. For
                 service in English, press 1.

Step 2:   Using the phone keypad, enter your account num-
                 ber, followed by the # sign.

Step 3:   Enter your password, followed by the # sign.

Step 4:   Press 2 for trading.

Step 5:   Press 2 for stock trades.

Step 6:   Press 1 to buy.

Step 7:   Enter the Nortel stock symbol (NT).

      Here's how to do this:

i)   N is on the sixth key of the phone keypad, so press 6.

ii)   N is in the second letter position of that key, so press 2.

iii)   T is on the eighth key, so press 8.

iv)   T is in the first letter position of that key, so press 1.

v)   Press the # sign.

Step 8:   Press 1, to signal a Canadian exchange. Automati-
                 cally, you will be given a real-time quote.

Step 9:   Enter the number of shares, followed by the # sign.

Step 10:   Press 2 for a limit order.

Step 11:   Enter the dollar portion of the price, followed by
                 the # sign

Step 12:   Enter the decimal portion of the price, followed by
                 the # sign.

Step 13:   Press 1 to signify a day order.

Step 14:   To place an order without restrictions, press 1.

Step 15:   Press 1 to settle in Canadian dollars.

A trade received over the automated phone line is then routed to a trader. If the trade is placed overnight, the information is held until morning when the traders come in. Assuming there are no mistakes, the order is then entered before the market opens. The same is true for discounters who offer Internet or PC-based trading but limit the hours that registered representatives work. Because nothing happens overnight, the trades are reviewed the following morning and scanned for mistakes.

Remember, what matters is when the order is entered by a trader not when the client places the order.

A NOTE ABOUT CIRCUIT BREAKERS

If the stock market takes a huge dive, circuit breakers will kick in to halt trading and permit a cooling-off period. The TSE has adopted the NYSE model for stopping trading. Here are the levels at which the circuit breakers cut in and the duration of the trading shutdown. The declines are measured as a percentage of the average closing value of the Dow Jones Industrial Average (DJIA) for the month preceding the quarter.

- A 10 per cent decline in the Dow Jones Industrial Average before 2 p.m. will shut the market for one hour.

- A 10 per cent decline in the Dow between 2 p.m. and 2:30 p.m. will shut the market for half and hour.

- A 10 per cent decline in the Dow after 2:30 p.m. will not shut the market.

- A 20 per cent decline in the Dow before 1 p.m. will shut the market for two hours.

- A 20 per cent decline in the Dow between 1 p.m. and 2 p.m. will shut the market for one hour.

- A 20 per cent decline in the Dow after 2 p.m. will close the market for the day.

- A 30 per cent decline in the Dow will automatically shut the market for the day.

Some Sample Stock Trades

Different markets and types of stocks call for different trading strategies. To help give you some ideas, we've put together four different scenarios and offered some tips.

Buying Amazon.com on a Busy Nasdaq Day

Nasdaq-traded Internet stocks like Amazon are notorious for their volatility. It's not out of the question for stocks like these to move up or down by $50 share or more in a single day. Normally, you'd use a limit order in this situation. But what if you really want to own this stock? In that case, don't mess around with a limit order. You may well end up undercutting the market price and not getting your order filled. You then might change your order and end up paying more than if you had used a market order in the first place. Something else to remember is that Nasdaq is a market where orders with restrictions often don't get filled, so avoid special terms on your order if possible. Note: Nasdaq is a market where you cannot submit Stop-Loss orders.

Trying to Sell Nortel Networks in a Major Pullback for the Stock

Nortel is the sort of stock that can do no wrong for a while, then gets slammed in the span of a few days on a change in investor sentiment that could be based on a variety of things, even rumour. If you absolutely must jettison the stock use a market order, but if you want to try and limit your losses, then use a stop-loss order. Once the stock hits the stop price, your order becomes a market sell. Or you could use a stop-limit order to place a minimum on the sale price.

Short Selling Corel Corp.

Corel stock tends to spike upward from time to time, even while the company faces skepticism about its corporate strategy and growth potential. It's this combination of factors that has drawn the attention of short sellers in the past. Most likely, you'll have to call your broker on the phone for short selling, which is a strategy for capitalizing on a price decline in a particular stock. With short selling, you borrow the stock and then buy it back when the price falls.

If you want to short a stock, you'll need to have your broker place a call to a floor trader and see if any of the shares can be borrowed from the firm's inventory or from another client who holds the stock. The client is then asked at what price he or she would like to sell. The margin requirements are between 130 and 150 per cent of the trade, which effectively means you have to top up the amount you receive from the sale by an additional 30 and 50 per cent. Significant danger exists if the account holder you borrowed the share from wants to sell them—the shares would be called in this case, meaning you'd have to buy the shares back regardless of where the price is. As well, if there are any dividends due, the short seller would be required to pay the dividend to the account holder from whom the shares were borrowed.

Buying TransCanada PipeLines in a Calm Market

TransCanada, traditionally a dividend play, is the kind of placid stock you can trade using market orders without worrying too much about being nailed by a sudden surge or retreat in the share price.

From the Trenches: Common Trading Blunders

We asked discount brokers what errors their clients made most often. Here they are:

- **Using a limit order instead of a market order and not getting an order filled:** If you want to invest cautiously and conservatively, then use limit orders. That way, you'll never pay more than what you want for a stock. Of course, you may not get the stock you want, especially if it's a high-flying issue in a fast-moving market. You have to make the call—do you really want the stock and the risk of paying a higher price than you initially anticipated? Or do you want to play it safe and possibly miss out?

- **Chasing a stock:** Let's say you used a limit order to try to buy a hot stock and you didn't get it filled. You change the order to a higher price, but the stock has outrun you and your order goes unfilled again. You then try again with yet another limit order at a higher price, but the result is the same. This is called chasing a stock and it's guaranteed to leave you feeling frustrated. Here's a possible solution: Why not place a market order for half the number of shares you wanted to buy initially? That way, if the stock rises, at least you've got a position and then you can determine whether to buy more. If the stock drops, then you can always "average down" by purchasing some more at a lower cost.

- **Using an all-or-none order when you really want a stock:** Hey, be a little flexible. Orders with restrictions have lower priority and sometimes don't get filled at all. A partial fill may be better than nothing.

- **Not knowing the depth of the market for market orders:** Here's something to be aware of if you use a market order and want to buy a large number of shares. Consider a scenario where you want 1,000 shares of a $6 stock. If only 100 shares were available at the $6 offered price, then the remaining number of shares would get executed at the next posted price, which is usually .05 or .10 more but can be quite a bit higher. If you enquired about depth, you'd know this and adjust the quantity of shares you're buying. If you went in blind, you could end up paying a lot more for the stock than expected.

- **Placing a market order before the stock market opens:** Unless you've got extremely deep pockets, placing a market order for a volatile stock before the 9:30 a.m. market opening can lead to disaster. A positive news release from late the previous day could push up the stock significantly at the open. If you expected the stock price to be around where it closed the previous day, you could be in for a shock.

- **Not following up on an order:** Submitting limit orders and then not watching to see what happens can lead to the disappointment of having an order go unfilled or only partially filled. Say you place a limit order for 1,000 shares of a $6 stock, then forget about it. At some point in the day, the order is placed at $6 exactly, but only 100 shares were purchased. The order for the remaining number of shares then expires at the end of the day. Result: You're angry at getting only a partial fill, especially when the broker got a full commission. If you had been monitoring things, though, you could have changed your limit order to a higher price so that the rest of the order could be filled.

- **Placing a trade on-line without confirming that it was received and reviewed:** Say you place a trade and walk away. You may find out later that the trade was rejected because there was a problem with it. The way to prevent this is to look at your broker order status screen and check what's happening with your order. What you're looking for is a notation that the trade is open (or that it has been executed). The term open means a broker has gone over the trade and has submitted it to the exchange floor. If the order status screen tells you your order is pending, that means it has yet to be reviewed. Your trade may also be listed as rejected, usually with no reason specified. Potential problems that would cause a trade to be rejected include insufficient funds, inappropriate restrictions and wrong account selected. Some brokers have you type in your phone number on the stock order screen so they can call if there's a problem. If a broker is very busy you may not get that phone call. Others will send an e-mail to advise you that your order was rejected (or filled).

- **Insufficient funds in the account:** This is a common reason trades are rejected. While you do normally have a few days to settle a trade, there are some circumstances where an order will be rejected if you don't already have the money in your account. For example, if the account has nothing in it, hasn't been traded within a year or is brand new, you may be required to have the money upfront.

- **Resubmitting an order without first checking whether it was filled:** It's a busy day on the markets and you go on-line to buy some shares. You submit the trade to your broker, but your screen freezes up and you're unsure whether the order was received at the other end. At this point some people will resubmit the trade, which is only a good move if you want to own double the amount of shares you originally intended. Before resubmitting an order, always make sure it was not received by your broker. Check the order status screen or use the telephone, if necessary.

What Happens After You Place a Trade

Let's deal with what doesn't happen first. When you hit the final OK for your on-line trade, it does not go right to the stock exchange floor for immediate execution. We repeat, on-line trading through a discount broker is not a direct pipeline into the markets.

Once an on-line order is received by a broker, it's quickly checked either manually or by a computer before being routed to the stock exchange. Primarily, the checks are designed to ensure you have either sufficient funds or sufficient margin in your account to cover the cost of your order.

Checking the Status of Your Order

If you trade by phone, you can call in to check on whether your order has been filled (this term applies to both buy and sell orders). Some brokers allow you to track phone orders through their Web site as well. Checking an order on a broker's Web site is a simple matter of looking for a button saying something like "order status."

When you click on this, you'll see a list of your current orders and a nearby column that tells you whether they are pending, which means awaiting vetting by a trader; open, which means awaiting execution; filled or partially filled. For partially filled orders, you'll be told how many shares have been bought or sold. Most brokers will let you see additional information on your order by clicking the a button that says something like "list details."

Changing or Cancelling an Order

If you're trading by telephone, always tell the trader whether you're cancelling or modifying an existing order (in broker lingo, this is called a CFO for change former order). If you're not clear about this, you could end up having two orders out there instead of one. On-line traders will find that modifying or cancelling an order is easily done just by clicking on the "cancel order" or "change order" buttons. If you're changing your order, you'll then go to a screen that is much like the original order page.

Obviously, order cancellations and modifications can only be made if the order has not been filled. That's what your broker means when it says all changes or cancellations are subject to prior fill. So, in theory and practice it is possible to have two orders executed on the same security. You may end up owning twice as many shares as you intended or, by selling twice as many, you may end up in a short position.

The Confirmation Slip

After your shares are purchased, your discounter will mail you a written notice of the trade containing:

- A description of the securities bought or sold.
- The price per share of the securities bought or sold.
- The currency the trade is executed in.
- The exchange the trade was placed on.
- The transaction and settlement dates of the transaction.
- The settlement amount, including the commission.
- The CUSIP number (CUSIP stands for Committee on Uniform Security Identification Procedures and acts as an identifier for all securities for easy identification for all levels of security transactions).

The confirmation slip is your official affirmation of purchase or sale—think of it it as your written receipt. Keep your slips because they can be useful for resolving disputes over trades and for calculating capital gains on your tax return.

On-line Trading Basics from the US Securities and Exchange Commission

On-line investing was riding a wave of phenomenal growth in May 1999 when SEC chairman Arthur Levitt gave a speech to the National Press Club in Washington in which he issued warnings to both investors and to brokers. Brokers, he said, should better inform clients about the realities of on-line trading. He also laid out four misconceptions that investors commonly have about on-line investing:

1. Personal computers are not directly linked to the markets: "Although the Internet makes it seem as if you have a direct connection to the securities market, you don't. Lines may clog; systems may break; orders may back up," Mr. Levitt said.

2. The virtue of limit orders: "Price quotes are only for a limited number of shares, so only the first few investors will receive the currently quoted price. By the time you get to the front of the line, the price of the stock could be very different. One way for investors to protect themselves from a rapid change in the price of a stock is to use a limit order rather than a market order."

3. Cancelling an order: "Another misconception is that an order is cancelled when you hit 'cancel' on your computer. But, the fact is that it's cancelled only when the market gets the cancellation. You may receive an electronic confirmation, but that only means that your request to cancel was received, not that your order was actually cancelled."

4. Buying on margin: "If you plan to borrow money to buy a stock, you also need to know the terms of the loan your broker gave you. This is called margin. In volatile markets, investors who put up an initial margin payment for a stock may find themselves required to provide additional cash if the price of the stock falls."

(Source: US Securities and Exchange Commission)

Basic Trading Strategies

Buy-and-Hold

This is investing at its most basic. You buy quality stocks or mutual funds and hang onto them for years, regardless of market fluctuations. All stocks and equity funds vary in price according to corporate earnings announcements, market hype, newspaper reports, upgrades and downgrades by analysts and for many other reasons. If you buy a strong company for the long term, none of these factors are of much importance. Some of the world's best known and successful investors are "buy-and-hold" types, for example, Warren Buffet.

Buy-and-hold investing has many things going for it when compared to active trading. One, you pay less in commissions. Two, you generally end up paying less in taxes because you're not triggering capital gains. Sell a stock that has increased in value and two-thirds of your capital gain will be taxed. There are no tax implications if the value of your portfolio increases on paper only. A third advantage of buy-and-hold investing is that there is less time and stress involved in managing the account.

There's no reason not to use a discount broker to set up a buy-and-hold portfolio, but it has to be noted that full-service dealers are a good option as well. It can take a lot of research and analysis to find stocks with real long-term growth potential. If you don't want to do this work, then you might find a full-service broker offers more value to you despite its far higher commissions.

**Setting up a Hypothetical Buy and Hold Portfolio
Using a Discount Broker**

Stocks	Commission Cost
100 shares BCE	$27*
100 shares Toronto-Dominion Bank	$27
50 shares Alcan	$27
50 shares Nortel Networks	$27
50 shares Barrick Gold	$27
100 shares Microsoft	US$40 (Cdn$60)
100 shares Gillette	US$40 (Cdn$60)
100 shares Ford	US$40 (Cdn$60)
50 shares Cisco Systems	US$40 (Cdn$60)
50 shares of Sony	US$40 (Cdn$60)

*average buy commission   TOTAL: Cdn$435

Speculating/Active Trading

Buy a stock cheap, ride it higher and dump it—this strategy takes the buy-low, sell-high axiom to another level. In this case often buy-high, sell-higher is appropriate. When the price falls, maybe you buy the stock back again in anticipation of another run-up. With their cheap commissions, discount brokers were made for this style of trading. You could execute dozens of on-line trades for the cost of just a handful done through a full-service dealer. Through its on-line services, a discounter also gives you much greater ability to manage and monitor your account. Note, however, than many investors have found they cannot momentum trade effectively during busy market periods because discount brokers can be slow to process and execute orders.

Here's an example of how a speculative play might work. After hitting the $100 range in the latter part of 1997, the on-line services provider Webco has bottomed out a few times around $30 and then shot into the $45 to $55 range. To capitalize on this pattern:

One – Submit a limit buy order for 500 shares of Webco at $30 and make it good for a month or as long as your broker will allow. If only a month, resubmit as necessary.

Two – When the buy order is filled, immediately place a stop limit order for the 500 shares at $51 with a limit of $50. Make it good for a month or longer if possible.

Three – Two months later, Webco shares have hit $50 and your position is sold out. Now place another limit buy order to start the process all over again.

Day Trading (or Short-Term Holds)

This is the polar opposite of buy-and-hold. You ignore the long-term growth potential of a company and instead focus on riding a wave of momentum over a span of time that is usually measured in minutes or hours. This strategy could involve using technical indicators to buy and sell or exploiting company news or economic developments.

Discount brokers are a rotten vehicle for day trading. Even on the best of days, there are no guarantees your trades will be executed fast enough to let you capitalize on intraday price movements. On bad days, when the market is crazy and Web trading systems are choking with traffic, day traders can find themselves cut off entirely from the market for stretches of an hour or more. Day traders also report that trade executions by discounters aren't as quick as they'd like, which often means more is paid for buy orders and less received for sell orders than would be possible with quicker action by a broker. Then there's the commissions. Discounters may be cheap in comparison with full-service operators, but they can still ding you hard if you trade continually.

If serious day trading is what you want to do, you should probably take a look at direct access trading through a firm like Toronto-based Swift Trade Securities Inc.. Services like this generally focus on the Nasdaq stock market, delivering client orders directly to the exchange for extra-quick execution. Swift Trade also offers training for day traders.

Leverage/Margin

Leverage is one of those terms that has taken on different meanings, but here it refers to the strategy of parlaying a small investment into a big return. How do you do this? The easiest way is to set up a margin account and use your discounter's money to help you buy a stock, bond or mutual fund. Generally, you can borrow 50 per cent of the cost of the stocks you're buying (70 per cent for option eligible stock). The other 50 per cent you put up yourself. This is what's known as the margin. Another benefit of margin investing is that the interest paid to the broker is usually tax deductible.

Figure 3: Buying 200 Shares of Toronto-Dominion Bank on Margin

---

TD Bank shares are trading at $50 and your broker will lend you up to 70 per cent of the cost of buying your shares.

Total invested	$10,000
Margin You Put Up	$3,000
Loaned By Your Broker	$7,000 (@ prime plus 1 percentage point—6%)

In six months' time, TD shares are trading at $60

Your shares are now worth	$12,000
Your gross return	$2,000 or 66% ($2,000 / $3,000 x 100)
Your borrowing costs are	$7,210 ($7,000 principal plus $210 interest)
Your net return is	$4,790 (58.8%)

Net return if you paid $10,000 in cash instead of buying on margin

Gross return $12,000 - $10,000
                 = $2,000 or 20% (12,000 -10,000/ 10,000)

Mutual funds tend to have 50 per cent margin, which means you put up half yourself and borrow the other half. If a fund portfolio of $10,000 increased to even $11,000, the return on an initial $5,000 investment would be 20 per cent before borrowing costs. The gain if the entire $10,000 were invested would be just 10 per cent. Don't forget that as a security bought on margin increases in value, so does the amount of money the broker is willing to lend. In this case you would be able to borrow an additional $500 (bringing the total borrowed amount to $5,500) based on the new portfolio value of $11,000.

Unfortunately, leverage can backfire big time if the value of the securities you bought falls. When this happens, the amount that the broker is willing to lend is pegged to the new value of the shares or fund units. Let's say your fund portfolio of $10,000 fell to $9,000, a 10 per cent drop in value. Your paper loss would actually be 20 per cent because you only put up $5,000. Meanwhile, because the value of the portfolio has decreased, the amount the broker is willing to lend has been pegged to the new value of the portfolio, $9,000. In this case, based on the 50 per cent loan maximum for mutual funds, the broker would only be willing to lend $4,500 (50 per cent of the remaining $9,000 in the portfolio). Originally you were lent $5,000; now your maximum is $4,500. Result: A margin call, which would be a request to put up an additional $500.

This is a comparatively mild example of a margin call. If there's a huge drop in the value of the fund portfolio or if you've borrowed heavily (the usual term is over-margined), then you might be forced to sell other securities to cover your obligations. If a stock in your portfolio dropped from $20,000 to $10,000 the amount your broker would lend would fall from $14,000 to $7,000 assuming the maximum 70 per cent loan was made. All of a sudden, you face a $7,000 margin call. The situation would be exacerbated if your broker decides to revise its maximum loan to say 50 per cent from the original 70 per cent. Then you would face a $9,000 margin call. That's the difference between the original loan of $14,000 and the new maximum of $5,000, which is 50 per cent of $10,000.

Leveraging can also mean buying shares or mutual fund units with money borrowed through a loan or a secured or unsecured line of credit. As with a margin loan, the potential gains and losses are magnified by the ratio of the loan to the value of the assets. However with bank loans, there is no risk of a margin call because the broker is not lending the money. The loan is based on your ability to repay it, not the value of the shares purchased.

For the most part, margin rules are set by the regulators, however, each broker reserves the right to limit how much they lend and to whom.

Dollar-Cost Averaging

This works great with mutual funds but generally not with stocks. With dollar-cost averaging, you buy securities in regular allotments instead of all at once. The idea is that you'll avoid being put in a position where you commit all your money and then watch the market tank. As well, buying in stages allows you to purchase more shares or units when prices are down while maintaining a structured investment plan when values are higher. The result is an acquisition price where the peaks and valleys are averaged out and the average price paid per unit is less than the highest price reached.

Dollar-cost averaging with stocks can be quite expensive even through a discounter since commissions would apply for each transaction. For this reason it is best used with mutual funds in conjunction with a preauthorized debit plan where a pre-set dollar amount is debited from a bank account every month and put into a particular fund. Whereas you'd pay a commission each time you bought a stock, funds can often be bought commission-free at a discounter.

As well, there have been academic studies that show you achieve higher returns by investing in one lump sum as opposed to in stages through dollar-cost averaging. However, the other side of the coin is that investing gradually is better than not being invested at all. Dollar-cost averaging can be described as a forced savings.

Averaging Down

This variation of dollar-cost averaging lets you take advantage of a price decline in a stock or fund you own to buy some more. If a mutual fund was originally bought at $10.00 per unit and subsequently dropped to $9.00, you could effectively reduce the average cost to $9.50 per unit by purchasing some more. This can be especially effective if the investment is a long-term hold. If you bought Newbridge Networks at $93 in the fall of 1997, you could have bought some more when they bottomed at $28 and driven down the average cost per share considerably. In doing so, you wouldn't have to wait for the stock to hit the $93 level to get back to a break-even position.

There's Trading and There's Over-Trading

Trading is a means to an end not an end in itself. Yet some investors get caught up in the excitement of being able to switch on their computer and almost instantly buy and sell stocks. They end up trading out of pure emotion, maybe because a stock they own is plunging one morning, or simply because they like the buzz they get from playing the market. Problem is, this can be detrimental to your investment returns. For one thing, heavy trading means heavy commissions. This is great for the broker, but bad for the investor because the accumulated costs can seriously bite into returns. If you buy and sell a stock twice a week and your broker charges a flat $29 commission, your cost will be $116 for the four transactions or $6,032 over the course of a year.

Investors who frequently flip their stocks may be hurting their returns in another way. Turning over stocks all the time is a form of market timing, which means trying to guess when a stock is at a low or high point. Most investors market time to some extent, but get too caught up in it and you might find that your trading is hurting as opposed to augmenting your returns.

And Then There's Obsessive Over-Trading

Aggressive speculative investing can in rare cases evolve into an unhealthy obsession or, worse, into a gambling addiction. Obviously, if you trade on-line through a discount broker, it's a lot easier to fall into this trap. Our point here is not to warn you about the dangers of investing too much, but more to make you aware that some people get carried away to the extent that they lose serious money or cause hurt to loved ones.

A group called the Connecticut Council on Problem Gambling offers a questionnaire on its Web site (**www.ncgambling.org**) to help make investors aware of the potential for problem gambling in financial markets. Here are the 20 questions followed by a explanation of how to interpret your score.

INVESTING AND GAMBLING PROBLEMS QUESTIONNAIRE

1. I have been preoccupied with seeking daily information about the status of my investments or trades or have been preoccupied with thoughts of past and future investments or trades.

    Yes   No

2. A major reason I have invested or traded is to change an unhappy mood, for example, escape worries, pressures, anxiety, depression etc.

    Yes   No

3. I have experienced extreme highs when I win and extreme lows when I lose in the markets.

    Yes   No

4. I have felt uncomfortable when any cash accumulated in my brokerage account and have needed to quickly find a way to keep it in action.

    Yes   No

5. I have been restless or irritable when unable to be active in the markets, for example, when short of money, away on vacation, trying to cut back on trades.

    Yes   No

6. I have needed to increase the amount invested or traded to maintain the high or excitement of being in action.
   Yes   No

7. My investments or trades have become increasingly speculative or risky over time.
   Yes   No

8. I have had more money at risk in the markets than I could afford to lose.
   Yes   No

9. I have often engaged in high volume investing or trading, for example, to outguess the direction of the market, etc.
   Yes   No

10. My investments or trades have been highly leveraged.
    Yes   No

11. I have not opened brokerage statements to avoid having to think about my losses.
    Yes   No

12. I have borrowed money from family, friends, credit cards or other sources to invest or trade.
    Yes   No

13. I have borrowed money to invest or trade and have not paid it back.
    Yes   No

14. I have had to have someone else provide money to relieve a crisis caused by my investing or trading.
    Yes   No

15. I have lied to people in order to hide that I was investing or trading or to hide how much money was involved.
    Yes   No

16. When losses have piled up, I continued the same investments and trades or increased the amount, in hopes my strategy would work or my luck would change and I would regain the losses.

    Yes   No

17. I have wanted to stop investing or trading but did not think I could, or I have been unsuccessful when I have tried to control, cut back or stop investing/trading.

    Yes   No

18. I have risked losing or lost important work, family or other commitments due to the amount of time and money taken up by my trading or investing.

    Yes   No

19. I have committed an illegal act to get money to continue to invest or trade or to pay back a loan for my investment activity.

    Yes   No

20. I have wondered whether I was gambling excessively in the markets.

    Yes   No

Scoring:

Yes answers:	No gambling problem
1-2 Yes answers:	Possible future problem.
3-4 Yes answers:	Mild current problem.
5-6 Yes answers:	Moderate current problem.
7 or more Yes answers:	Severe current problem.

Reprinted with permission from the Connecticut Council on Problem Gambling, Inc.
http://www.ncpgambling.org/ccpg/investing.html

A Few Things You Should Know

There's more to owning stocks that just watching them go up in value (hopefully), especially if you deal with a discounter and thus don't have anyone to explain to you about how dividends work or what to do if there's an offer to take over a company whose stock you hold. Here's a quick rundown on what happens in such situations.

Dividends

Common and preferred share dividends are usually paid out on a quarterly basis and deposited into your brokerage account as cash, unless you have a dividend reinvestment plan (see Chapter Ten). You can also arrange to have your dividends paid into a bank account linked to your brokerage account.

The date you purchased your shares is the key for determining if you're entitled to a dividend. What you need to look out for is the record date declared by the company that issued the stock in question. If you bought your shares before the record date, you're entitled to receive the dividend, but if you bought after that date, no dividends for you.

Keep in mind that it takes three business days to settle a stock trade, which means that a trade placed on Monday would settle on Thursday (assuming no holidays). Now, say a company set June 4th as its record date. If you wanted to ensure you were entitled to that dividend, you would take that date and count back three days. In other words, you would have to buy the shares by June 1st to receive the dividend. After June 1, the shares would be said to be trading ex dividend meaning without the dividend. Before June 1, they're trading cum dividend or with dividend.

Stock Splits

When a company feels that its share price is too high, and it implements a stock split, your discount broker will automatically adjust your account. The same holds in the case of a reverse split, where two or more shares are consolidated into one.

Mergers, Takeovers and Reorganizations

Let's say you hold the stock of a company that is the subject of a takeover offer. You should receive an information package from the company whose stock you hold explaining the details of the offer along with instructions on whether to vote for or against the offer. Next, your discounter will contact you by telephone to take your instructions on whether to tender or not. If the takeover is successful, it can take several weeks after the deal closes until tendering shareholders receive the money or shares they were offered in the transaction.

Stock Markets

Here's a rundown on all the major Canadian and US stock exchanges and indexes, including a brief explanation of how they work. You can use this information in two ways, one being to familiarize yourself with lesser-known exchanges where you may be buying stocks through your discount account. As well, knowing how a particular exchange works will help you effectively use stock exchange performance numbers to benchmark the returns of your own portfolio.

Key Canadian Indexes

TSE 300 Composite Index: A key benchmark for stock market performance in Canada, the TSE 300 consists of 14 industry groups and 33 subgroups. It's a market value weighted index, which means that stocks with a high market capitalization (share prices multiplied by the number of shares outstanding) will have a larger impact on overall market performance.

S&P/TSE 60 Index: The stocks in this index have been chosen from among the TSE 300 stocks for their size, liquidity and sector leadership. There are 11 sectors in the S&P/TSE 60.

S&P/TSE Canadian SmallCap Stock Index: This benchmark for small-cap investing consists of the smallest companies in each of the sectors in the TSE 300 index.

S&P/TSE Canadian MidCap Stock Index: An index of 60 stocks picked for their liquidity and designed to represent companies that fall between the previous two indexes.

TSE 35 Index: Thirty-five of the country's largest corporations are included in this index, which was designed to track the TSE 300 index. The TSE 35 has been de-emphasized with the introduction of the S&P/TSE 60.

TSE 100 Index: A slimmed down version of the TSE 300 designed as a benchmarket for institutional investors like pension funds. It also faces redundancy because of the S&P/TSE 60.

CDNX Index: This is the key index of the Canadian Venture Exchange, launched in 1999 out of the merger of the Vancouver Stock Exchange and the Alberta Stock Exchange. The CDNX Index represents 80 per cent of the total market capitalization of all index-eligible securities.

Canadian Market Portfolio Index (XXM): The key index on the Montreal Exchange is intended to reflect the performance of the country's largest stocks. It consists of 25 large-capitalization stocks that are listed on at least two stock exchanges.

Key US Indexes

AMEX Composite: This is a capitalization-weighted index (it gives greater weight with stocks having greater market value) of all stocks trading on the American Stock Exchange.

Dow Jones Average of 30 Industrials: This may be the most followed index the world. It measures the performance of 30 corporate behemoths.

NASDAQ Composite: All the stocks that trade on the Nasdaq. It accounts for 15 per cent of the US market.

NASDAQ 100: This index includes the 100 largest non-financial stocks on the NASDAQ exchange.

NYSE Composite: This is a capitalization-weighted index of all stocks trading on the New York Stock Exchange.

Russell 2000: The index is designed to be a comprehensive representation of the US small-cap equities market.

Standard & Poor's 500: These 500 stocks include 400 industrial stocks, 20 transportation stocks, 40 utility and 40 financial. It represents about 70 per cent of US stock market.

Standard & Poor's 400 (aka **S&P Midcap**)**:** This index tracks 400 industrial stocks.

Standard & Poor's 100 (and OEX): The S&P 100 is an index of 100 stocks. The OEX is the option on this index, one of the most heavily traded options around.

Value Line Composite: This is a price-weighted index as opposed to a capitalization index.

Wilshire 5000: The Wilshire 5000 consists of all US-headquartered companies. This index actually now includes over 7,000 companies.

Other Indexes:

CAC-40 (France)
The 40 stocks on the Paris Stock Exchange formed into an index. The futures contract on this index is probably the most heavily traded futures contract in the world.

DAX (Germany)
The German share index DAX tracks the 30 most heavily traded stocks (based on the past three years of data) on the Frankfurt exchange.

FTSE-100 (Great Britain)
Commonly known as "footsie," it consists of a weighted arithmetical index of 100 leading UK equities by market capitalization. Calculated on a minute-by-minute basis, the footsie basically represents the bulk of the UK market activity.

Nikkei (Japan)
Nikkei is an abbreviation of *nihon keizai*—*nihon* is Japanese for Japan, while *keizai* is business, finance, economy etc. Nikkei is also the name of Japan's version of the *Wall Street Journal*. The Nikkei is sometimes called the Japanese Dow in that it is the most popular and commonly quoted Japanese market index.

JPN (Japan)
JPN is a modified price-weighted index that measures the aggregate performance of 210 common stocks actively traded on the Tokyo Stock Exchange that are representative of a broad cross-section of Japanese industries. JPN is closely related to the Nikkei Index, but they are not identical. Options are traded on US exchanges.

Europe, Australia, and Far East (EAFE)
Compiled by Morgan Stanley, this is a a benchmark index for key markets outside North America.

DID YOU KNOW?

On almost any given day larger Nasdaq and NYSE stocks such as Microsoft, CISCO and IBM will trade more than the entire TSE.

Stock Market Web Resources

Stock Exchanges

www.tse.com (Toronto Stock Exchange): Very detailed stock quotes, plus P/E ratios and dividend yields for listed stocks and an exhaustive look at the operations of Canada's senior stock exchange. A portfolio tracker lets you follow 25 TSE-listed companies and mutual funds, while a shopping area sells investing books and trinkets.

www.cdnx.com (Canadian Venture Exchange): A clean, fast-moving site that tells all about the country's small-cap stock market. You can find data on the day's trading, as well as member company information and quotes.

www.me.org (Montreal Exchange): A decent rundown on the country's centre of derivative trading, but it contains some dated information as well.

www.nyse.com (New York Stock Exchange): The world's most important stock market gets the Web treatment it deserves. This beautiful site explains the NYSE's operations and offers a portfolio tracker for stocks and stock indexes.

www.nasdaq.com (Nasdaq): The emphasis on this excellent site is on helping investors find out about listed stocks. Quotes and charting are available, as are analyst rating summaries, company news, fundamentals and regulatory filings. If you want to research a Nasdaq-listed stock, don't miss this Web site.

www.amex.com (American Stock Exchange): This site has a similar design to Nasdaq's, which isn't surprising since the two are operated in tandem.

indexes.dowjones.com (Dow Jones Indexes): This site offers information on the Dow Jones average of 30 industrials, plus other Dow indexes.

www.site-by-site.com (International Stock Markets): A Web site with a rather mundane name, Site-By-Site has compiled an international investing database that includes links to all the world's major stock markets. Looking for the Warsaw, Helsinki or Taipei stock exchanges? You'll be able to find them here easily.

Daily Stock Market and Business News Updates

www.bay-street.com: This is an eclectic mix of investing resources, including business headlines, North American and global market updates, audio news reports from CBC, daily commentary from financial writer Garth Turner and investing newsletter previews. (Canadian site).

www.bloomberg.com: This site is a vast reservoir of business and market news from around the world (US site)

www.bridge.com: Here you will find global market coverage that you can customize according to the countries or markets you want to follow. If you choose Canada, you can get detailed quotes on TSE-listed companies. You have to register for the basic service, but it's free. (US)

www.briefing.com: Briefing.com has respected analysis on stock and bond market trends. Some free stuff is available but most is reserved for paying subscribers. (US)

www.canoe.ca/money/home.html: The Canoe Web site's money section carries market and financial news from the Canadian Press and Reuters. (Cdn)

www.cbc.ca/business: The CBC's business page is a great resource for checking on daily market and business news plus reading personal finance features. Some material is available in audio and video format. (Cdn)

www.cbs.marketwatch.com: Scan the CBS headlines, look at a summary of the day's news, or type in a stock symbol and see what news comes up. Also, there is lots of market commentary and personal finance content. (US)

www.cnbc.com: This site offers news but also commentary and analysis on the markets, individual stocks and personal finance matters. There are awesome some stock research tools as well. (US)

www.cnnfn.com: The business page of the CNN Web site offers a good mix of market updates and business news. (US)

www.dowjones.com: The Dow Jones site has news on the markets, business, economics and personal finance. (US)

www.imoney.com: Reuters business headlines are offered on the this personal finance/investing site. (Cdn)

www.intermoney.com: This site has global market, economic and currency coverage. You have to register, but it's free. (US)

www.investcom.com: A newer site that combines market news with a group of features that include articles from investing newsletters and stock research tools. (Cdn)

www.investorsalley.com: The Investors Alley site provides market and business news as well as lots of features and commentary. (US)

www.msnbc.com: The business section of this site combines CNBC business material with stories from the *Wall Street Journal* (US).

www.mworld.com: Macro World's site tracks markets around the world and includes research on US companies. (US)

www.quicken.ca: This all-purpose personal finance/investing site has business headlines and market summaries from the Canadian Press and Reuters as well as news releases of the day. (Cdn)

www.quote.com: This is a good site for keeping tabs on the US market during the day. It is owned by Lycos, Inc. Market wrap-ups and individual news stories are available along with news, listings of analyst upgrades/downgrades and positive earnings surprises. (US)

www.quoteserver.com: This site features detailed looks at the NYSE, Amex and Nasdaq, including technical lists like stocks falling below their 200-day moving average. (US)

www.reuters.com: Reuters offers daily global financial news available on the business section of this site. (Global)

www.smallcapcentre.com: This specialist in small-caps traded on North American exchanges has a staff of writers who produce updates and features throughout the trading day. It includes research tools as well plus a sophisticated portfolio tracker. (Cdn)

www.stockhouse.com: The StockHouse site includes news releases plus news reports from the Canadian Press, Reuters and CNNfn and has stock bulletin boards and newsletters as well. (Cdn)

7

Buying Mutual Funds Through a Discount Broker

There's no question that the glamour in the discount brokerage business is in trading stocks, but don't for a moment think that discounters aren't interested in clients who prefer mutual funds, because that is far from the truth. Discounters want your fund business and they're going after it aggressively by lowering commissions, continually expanding their fund offerings and providing free research tools that help clients pick funds. Some discounters even offer a limited amount of advice to novice clients looking for help in choosing appropriate funds.

The reason why discounters are courting fund investors is simple—trailer fees. As the seller of a mutual fund, discount brokers get paid a yearly fee from fund companies as compensation for the ongoing service and administration they provide to fundholders. A trailer fee for a typical Canadian equity fund would be 1 per cent per year, which translates into $500 on a $50,000 portfolio. Multiply that by hundreds of thousands of investors and you understand why selling mutual funds is a rewarding business, even if it isn't as sexy as equities.

There are good reasons to buy funds through a discounter, including the fact that many of them have removed just about all costs associated with buying a mutual fund. Centralization is another good reason, particularly when it comes to RRSP accounts. Rather than having a few funds with your bank and some more in separate accounts with a few odd fund companies here and there, you can have all your funds parked in a single discount broker account. That will mean one account statement and one RRSP administration fee instead of many. In fact, you may not have any fee since some brokers no longer charge them.

Selection is another reason to buy funds through a discount broker. Many discounters offer somewhere around 1,000 funds from both their affiliated bank (if they have one) and from third-party fund companies that range from powerhouses like Mackenzie, Fidelity, Templeton and Trimark to smaller operators like Bissett and Elliott & Page.

Want to know if your broker sells a fund that interests you? First, check the broker's Web site. If you can't find the information there, call and ask to speak to a fund specialist. Calling a specialist is a good idea, anyway, since brokers are adding new funds to their rosters all the time and not always posting the information on their Web sites.

The large selection of funds offered by most brokers pays off by allowing you to easily cherry pick the best funds from a variety of companies for your portfolio. If you're considering buying funds through one of those commission-free, funds-only dealers like Altamira's Mutual Fund Direct, be sure to check the range of funds offered. It probably won't be as wide a selection as a discount broker offers.

In one case, buying a mutual fund on-line means that you will pay a lower MER (management expense ratio) than if you purchased it any other way. That's the marketing hook that Toronto-Dominion Bank introduced in late 1999 with its index funds. Bought over the Internet, these eFunds, as they're called, have fabulously low MERs of between 0.29 per cent and 0.45 per cent. That compares to between .80 per cent and .90 per cent for the same funds bought through traditional channels. The catch here is that TD's eFunds are available only over the Internet from either the bank or its discount brokerage arm, TD Waterhouse. It's possible that other discounters will start offering TD's eFunds (the bank's other funds will almost certainly be offered at most discounters), so be sure to check if you're interested in index funds.

That's the good news story on discounters and funds. The bad is that there are all kinds of tiny fees, exclusions and exceptions that keep cropping up to confuse and confound investors. A broker might, for example, sell a particular fund but require a higher minimum initial investment than the fund company specifies in its prospectus. Or maybe the no-load fund you want isn't available without a front-load commission because the fund company offering it doesn't pay trailer fees. As we saw in Chapter Five, there's also a maddening array of fees that can be slapped on mutual fund accounts.

The lesson here is to call your discounter on the phone before buying anything and ask:

- Do they sell the fund you want to buy?
- Are there any account set-up fees?
- What is the minimum initial investment, the minimum subsequent investment and the minimum for pre-authorized chequing plans? These may be determined by the fund company.
- Does any front-load commission apply (ask this even for no-load funds*)?

Getting Ready to Buy a Mutual Fund

Mutual funds are simpler to buy than stocks, but there's still some advance work you have to do as a discount broker client who isn't receiving any guidance. For instance, you may know the name of the fund you want to buy, but do you have the right version of that fund? The mutual fund world has gone crazy lately developing different twists on the same essential fund. You

---

* Some discount brokers will have a commission fee of up to 2 per cent on no-load fund that do not pay trailer fees such as Bassett and Phillips, Hager & North.

might have a regular version, a segregated fund version (which provides limited guarantees for your principal), or a RRSP-eligible version and US-dollar version if it's a foreign fund. For example, the Templeton International Stock Fund comes in four variations, and the Trimark Fund comes in three.

If you're buying a load fund, then there's also the question of whether it's a front-load or a back-end load, also called a deferred sales charge or DSC fund. With a front-load fund, you pay a small percentage of your capital upfront and then you can bail out of the fund at any time with no further commissions from the fund company (although your broker may charge you an exit fee). A DSC fund, on the other hand, charges you nothing upfront, but you'll pay a commission to redeem the fund any time in the first six or seven years you own it. Usually, the redemption fee starts at somewhere around six or seven per cent and then declines steadily to zero.

Most discounters have waived their commissions on front-load funds, which means front-load funds and no-load funds are now one and the same at these establishments. Given this development, you might wonder why anybody in their right mind would buy a DSC fund, with it's penalties for cashing out in the years after buying in. One reason—not a good one, but still a reason—is that some discounters offer small bonuses to clients who buy DSC funds of up to 3 per cent of their investment capital. The bonus may add up for large investments, but your freedom to move fund companies without facing redemption penalties is worth more.

Placing the Buy Order

When buying funds over the telephone, the trader will ask for the amount you want to invest, the fund name and, if it's a load fund, whether you want a front load or DSC. If you choose a front load and a commission applies, you'll be asked if you want to pay the commission separately or have it come out of the capital you're investing. If you buy a fund on-line, you'll usually have to provide a fund symbol. These are like stock symbols, except that nobody knows them off the top of their head. Don't worry, the fund order screen will provide you with a search engine to look up the right fund symbol. Be careful to get the symbol right—front load and DSC versions of the same fund will have symbols that are just slightly different. Another question in buying funds is whether you want your dividends and distributions reinvested or whether you want to take them out in cash. Going the reinvestment route means you'll periodically be buying new units in your fund.

In addition to buying and selling funds, you can make switches between funds in the same family. For instance, you might sell out of the Trimark Fund, a global offering, and put the proceeds into the Trimark Discovery Fund, which focuses on technology- and innovation-based companies. Some brokers will let you make a switch for free, while others will charge a fee that can be as high as $40. If you hold a DSC fund, you should be able to switch into another fund in the same family without triggering any redemption fees. Some DSC funds will also allow you to redeem up to 10 per cent of your holdings per year without triggering a penalty fee.

If you're buying funds as your first trade, be warned that you might be asked to have the capital you're investing in your account at the time you place your order. Otherwise, it takes three days for a fund trade to be settled.

DID YOU KNOW?

Canadian mutual funds are valued once a day while many US mutual funds are valued more often than that. Canadian discounters require that a trade be placed often before 2:00 p.m. to receive a fund's current day closing valuation. Otherwise, the next day's valuation would be used and a significant price difference may occur.

Getting Help

Recognizing that funds are often an entree into the investing world, most discounters have taken the step of providing a limited amount of help to people choosing mutual funds. The usual procedure is to call the broker and ask to speak to a mutual fund specialist who then asks you about such details as your age and risk tolerance. Fund advisers won't recommend specific funds, but they might be able to help you narrow down a wide selection of funds into a small list of possible choices. They should also be able to supply research or background reports on specific funds and suggest an asset allocation model (i.e.: what portion of your portfolio should go into equity funds, fixed income funds and so on). All brokers but E*Trade Canada, HSBC and Scotia offer some assistance. Here's a summary of the discount brokers that offer fund assistance:

Bank of Montreal InvestorLine: Fund specialists will provide information on your funds and help you use the discounter's on-line mutual fund research tools.

Charles Schwab Canada: Clients have the option of working with an investment advisor at Schwab, which means they can get advice on funds as well as any other type of security. The cost is substantially higher commissions, including a charge of 2 per cent for buying front-load funds.

CIBC Investor's Edge: The CIBC Investor Services Mutual Fund Desk will help you get a prospectus or any other information related to the funds sold by the discounter.

CT Securities: Mutual fund specialists can help you find information on funds that interest you.

Disnat: Clients can call in for help using Disnat's Mutual Fund Selection Service, which helps locate funds that meet your investing objectives.

National Bank Discount Brokerage: The Mutual Fund Advisory Service will help clients assess their needs, choose funds and determine a proper asset mix.

Royal Bank Action Direct: Fund specialists will talk to you on the telephone and help you make your way through the broad selection of funds out there, evaluate the performance of your existing funds and help you find access to independent expert opinions on funds.

Sun Life Securities: Sun Life's brokers are geared toward answering even basic questions about mutual funds like the difference between front- and back-end loads.

TD Waterhouse: The FundSmart Service will either provide you with details on specific funds or suggest one of several possible portfolios from the Green Line Managed Assets Program, which are composed of different combinations of funds from the Green Line fund family.

Mutual Fund Web Resources

www.canoe.ca/money/home.html: The Canoe money site has a fund section with news, daily performance numbers and research tools.

www.fundlibrary.com: The Fund Library is great for researching funds, keeping up on industry news or for chatting with other investors about funds and other investing issues on the Fund Library Discussion Forum.

www.fundcounsel.com (Fund Counsel Newsletter): One of the best-looking fund sites offers features and analysis on the fund world. There's also some interesting quirky stuff like Battle of the Funds, which pits two similar funds against each other.

www.globefund.com: This is the best site out there for researching mutual funds, period. Great graphing and charting features.

www.ific.ca (Investment Funds Institute of Canada): This is the place to go to learn about basic fund industry terms and issues.

www.imoney.com: This personal finance/investing site has the de rigueur section on mutual funds.

www.investcom.com: The fund section of this general investing site ties a number of tools from other sources together into a nice package. Charts from Globefund, daily price updates from Fund Library, and fund summaries from Morningstar Canada (formerly Portfolio Analytics).

www.investorlearning.ca (The Investor Learning Centre): Mutual fund basics with a cut-through-the-bull approach. Check out the material on alternatives to mutual funds.

www.morningstar.ca (Morningstar Canada): Morningstar is the pre-eminent mutual fund rater in the United States and its new Canadian Web site is stuffed with features and analysis, as well as fund ratings on a 5 star scale. Also, check at Morningstar's U.S. Web at **www.morningstar.com**.

www.quicken.ca: A good selection of basic information about funds, as well as research tools, columns and analysis on fund issues.

8

Buying Bonds Through a Discount Broker

The bond market has none of the glamour of the stock market, even though by some estimates it's 35 times larger. At the average discount broker, the emphasis on stocks over bonds is even more striking than it is elsewhere in the investing world. Let's face it, most investors sign up with a discounter to trade stocks not buy bonds. No one chooses a discounter because it has the best fixed-income desk or because it offers the best bond analysis tools or research. CT Securities has a client base with one of the highest bond allocations out there at just 17 per cent of total assets. E*Trade Canada customers are at the opposite end of the scale with just 2 per cent of their assets in bonds.

> **WHAT IS A BOND?**
>
> A bond is a certificate of debt secured by certain assets of a company, or in the case of government issues, the ability to raise money through taxes. For example, you may find that a manufacturing company has issued bonds and used the plant equipment as security for the debt, or that a financial service company may have issued debt based on the proprietory software it has developed. If a bond is unsecured, then technically it is a debenture.

Discount brokers definitely expect their clients to buy more bonds in the future. In part, this is because discounters realize that the stock market is bound to go into a slump sometime, and when it does investors will likely become more interested in bonds. As well, discounters realize that their business will become more mainstream in the future. Where hard-trading stock investors are the main discount broker customers now, in the future they're likely to be mainstream types who want a balanced approach that requires a mix of stocks and bonds.

Getting Ready

The most important thing to know about choosing a bond to invest in is that it is much easier than selecting a stock. With stocks, you have to consider the economic sector the issuing company is in, the financial strength of the company and the stock's recent trading patterns, just to name a few factors. With bonds, there's a lot less to worry about. In fact, you'll likely find that there are several different bonds that meet your investing criteria with not much to recommend one over the other beyond a few basis points of yield (a basis point is a one-hundredth of a percentage point) or a credit rating that is a slight gradation higher.

What follows is a list of criteria for selecting a bond, tailored for discount broker clients. Whereas a full-service broker will walk you through these points, a fixed-income specialist at a discounter will expect you to have a fair understanding of each point.

- **The Issuer:** Is the bond issued by Fly-By-Night Corp., or the government of Canada? You get more yield, or a higher interest rate payout, the lower you go in credit quality (for example, junk bonds), but you also get more risk of default. A provincial government or high-grade corporate bond may give a good trade-off between yield and risk. More and more investors are buying corporate bonds as a result of the fact that, with government debt levels declining in Canada, the supply of federal and provincial government bonds is slowly declining.

- **Credit Quality:** All bonds are assigned a credit rating by one or more of the major bond-rating services. The ratings address the creditworthiness of the issuer, or the likelihood that investors will receive their interest payments without a risk of default. Triple-A bonds are the safest and anything rated triple-B or higher is considered investment grade, suitable for conservative investors like pensions funds. Some funds won't go below single-A, however.

Figure 1: Sample Bond Ratings

Canadian Bond Rating Service's Rating Scale for Long-Term Government Bonds*		
Highest Quality	AAA	investment grade†
Very Good Quality	AA	investment grade
Good Quality	A	investment grade
Medium Quality	BBB	investment grade
Lower Medium Quality	BB	medium
Poor Quality	B	risky
Speculative Quality	C	speculative
Default	D	default second tier

†each category may be further broken down into high and low ratings.

*Dominion Bond Rating Service has a similar rating system.

- **Term:** The term on the bond refers to the length of time until it matures. When issued, a bond may have a 30-year maturity, but five years later, it's a 25-year bond. You have complete freedom to pick a term, but you also have to be flexible in making your wants correspond with the terms of the bonds your broker has in its inventory. For instance, you might want a five-year bond that matures in June 2006. Your broker might only be able to deliver something that comes due in August or September.

- **Yield to Maturity:** If you hold a bond until it matures, this is the annual rate of return you would theoretically receive. Obviously, you want as high a yield as you can get within the confines of your needs on term and credit quality. Note that yield is different than coupon, a term that refers to the annual interest rate on the bond at the time of issue.

- **Strip and Standard Bonds:** A detailed description of strips follows at the end of this chapter, but their key feature is that they don't pay interest annually (they've been stripped of their coupons, hence the name). Instead, you buy them at a discount and then collect the face value at maturity. Standard bonds, on the other hand, pay interest semi-annually in most cases and then pay out the face value (par) at maturity. A $1,000 20-year bond with a 6 per cent coupon would pay $30 every six months and the $1,000 principal at maturity, whereas a strip bond would be sold at, say, $311.81 and mature at $1,000 in 20 years.

- **Amount You Want to Invest:** Bonds can usually be bought in increments of as little as $5,000, although some brokers may offer batches as small as $1,000.

As an example, you might decide you want a bond with a maturity of 10 years, a yield of roughly 6 per cent, a single-A rating or better and be issued by a provincial government or government agency such as a hydro utility. Further specifications could include that the bond be denominated in German marks or US dollars.

DID YOU KNOW?

Long-term bonds are those that have a maturity of longer than 10 years and often up to 25 or 30 years, while medium-term bonds go from three to 10 years; short-term bonds mature in less than three years.

Placing the Buy Order

On-line bond trading arrived in Canada in late 1999 when a small outfit called E-bond—**www.e-bond.ca**—opened up for business. Around the same time, TD Waterhouse announced it would be offering on-line bond trading to its US business first and then to its Canadian operation in the first half of 2000. Most other discounters expect to be trading bonds on-line sometime in 2000. On-line bond trading will allow you to browse through a selection of bonds on your broker's secure Web site, then purchase them electronically, just as you would a stock, mutual fund or option.

For now, though, most discount clients must still buy their bonds over the telephone. Dial your broker's 1-800 number and ask to speak to the bond or fixed-income desk. Next, give the representative your wish list in terms of issuer, term, credit quality and so on. The rep will then check his or her inventory to see what's there that can fill your requirements. Some brokers can also shop around at other dealers to find a bond you want.

WHAT NOT TO DO

Check the bond listings in the business section of your daily newspaper and pick something from there to buy. Many of those bond issues are very illiquid, which means they trade little if at all. The net result is that your discounter may not be able to buy them for you.

In describing what's available to meet your requirements, a broker will tell you both the yield to maturity and the price for a bond. Bond yields fluctuate throughout the day just like stock prices, so the quote you get at 9 a.m. may not be the same if you call back after lunch (remember: bond prices and yields move in opposite directions). The price and yield you actually receive will be the ones set at the time you place your order.

After your broker lays out the bond choices available that meet your specifications, you'll usually select the one with the highest yield. Once you've decided what you want, the investment representative will place the order. The quoted price is the price paid—there are no extra commissions to be paid because they have already been worked into the price.

Buying a Bond

Your discount broker's bond inventory might look something like this (we've kept the list to federal and provincial government issues only):

Amount Available and Issuer	Coupon	Maturity	Price	Yield
**4,051,000 CDA	5.5	06/01/2010	96.202	6
923,000 QUE	10	06/28/2010	126.301	6.466
888,000 PEI	11.5	08/16/2010	137.625	6.489
958,000 CDA	9	03/01/2011	123.008	6.098
3,744,000 BC	9.5	01/09/2012	125.46	6.401
210.000 MA	8.5	07/22/2013	118.922	6.377

** After hearing what's avialable, you choose this Government of Canada bond. To buy $10,000 worth would cost $9,620.20 (cost of $96.202 per $100 of face value). The bond's yield, or annual interest payout, is 6 per cent. Commission is included in the price quoted to you.

Sample Bond Trade

Client: Hello. I'd like to buy a bond, please.

Agent: What's your name and account number?

Client: 222- 222-22 B

Agent: Very good, then. I'll pass you through to our bond desk and they'll be able to assist you further.

New agent: Hello, Mr. Smith?

Client: Yes, I'm interested in balancing out my existing portfolio with some bonds or other fixed-income investments.

Agent: Certainly, I can help you. What type of fixed-income security did you want short, medium or long term?

Client: Well, actually I was looking for something medium term in the 7 percent yield range. What do you have that might fit?

Agent: Let me see. I've got a 10-year corporate issued by Loblaw Cos. Ltd. with a double-A rating, 6 per cent coupon and 6.96 yield to maturity. What do you think?

Client:	That sounds great, now what's the price on it?
Agent:	The price is $104.58 for every $100 of face value. How much did you want to invest?
Client:	About $5,000.
Agent:	OK. Then your cost of this bond would be $5,229.

A Few Bond Tips for Discount Broker Clients

If you want to become an expert on bonds, check out the Web sites listed at the end of this chapter, or visit the investing section of a good bookstore. For starters, take a look at the information that follows. What we've done is take a few bond terms and explain them so that you can be a more effective do-it-yourself bond investor.

> **THREE RULES TO HEED WHEN INVESTING IN BONDS:**
>
> 1. Bond prices and bond yields are inversely related. So when interest rates rise bond prices fall and vise versa.
> 2. Long bonds are more volatile than shorter term ones
> 3. Low coupon bonds are more volatile than higher coupon ones.

Now, a few key terms and techniques for bond investors:

Laddering

If you buy bonds that are rated highly by the bond-rating agencies, what risks are there? Let's consider what would happen if you had a $10,000 five-year bond that paid 10 per cent annual interest. For sure, you'd be happy knowing that for each year you held the bond, you'd receive 10 per cent of your principal in income. But what happens when this bond matures and you find that the comparable rate now is 4 per cent. You've gone from 10 per cent to 4 per cent, or from $1,000 to $400/year, which can be quite a shock.

Here's what to do. Instead of putting all your money down on a bond with a 10-year term, for example, break up it up into five segments invested in terms ranging from one to five years. By doing this, you'll be able to limit your exposure to a drop in interest rates, and have fresh money available every year to take advantage of higher rates. This is similar to the dollar-cost averaging strategy with mutual funds.

Strip Bonds

A strip is essentially a bond with all the coupon payments clipped off, which is why they're sometimes called zero-coupon bonds. Instead of receiving semi-annual interest payments, strips are bought at a discount and then redeemed at their face value at maturity. The difference between the discount and the face value is used to calculate a notional annual interest payout or yield.

An important detail about strips is that they're best held in RRSPs. The reason is that strips are considered to pay interest annually and taxed accordingly. Outside an RRSP, then, a strip would generate an annual tax bill even though it doesn't produce any true returns until maturity. Another thing to watch out for with strips is their volatility. Prices can swing wildly, following the course of interest rates, which means you could end up with a capital gain or loss if you sold a strip before maturity. Remember Rule #3 above, low coupon bonds are more volatile than high coupon bonds and by definition strip bonds have no coupon. If you hang on until maturity, the prices fluctuations are meaningless.

Treasury Bills

These are very short-term securities that, like strip bonds, are purchased at a discount and redeemed at par. They're issued by governments (usually federal) and discount broker clients can usually buy them in units of as little as $1,000 par value (maturity value). T-bills are issued withn three-, six- and nine-month maturities.

Accrued Interest

Bond interest payments are generally made twice a year, which means you could quite easily buy a bond that is between payments. Who collects the interest accrued prior to the sale, you or the seller? The answer is the seller. Say a bond has semi-annual interest payments on June 30 and Dec. 31. If you buy this bond on Jan. 31, the seller of the bond would be entitled to interest accrued up to Jan. 31. This payment to the seller would be factored into the purchase price of the bond and be invisible to you, the buyer.

Web Resources for Bond Investors

Bond Rating Agencies

www.dbrs.com (Dominion Bond Rating Service)
www.dsuper.net/~cbrs/page1.htm (Canadian Bond Rating Service)
www.moodys.com (Moody's Investors Service)

On-line Bond Trading, Quotes

www.e-bond.ca (E-Bond on-line bond trading)
www.canpx.ca (CanPX)

Research/Learning

www.investinginbonds.com (The Bond Market Association)
www.personalwealth.com (Standard & Poor's)

9

Options

Options trades are for people with significant investing experience and a strong tolerance for risk. When placing a trade, you have to know all the applicable, appropriate terms. For example, you have to know whether you're interested in puts or calls, the expiry, the strike price of the option contract and the spread between bid and asked values. Open interest and sizing are terms with particular relevance to options traders, as are exercise and automatic exercise.

Option Quotes

Bid and ask are really the same things here as they are for equity trades. Bid refers to the highest price someone is willing to pay for a board lot of contracts for a specific exercise or strike price of an option contract, and the ask is the price at which someone is willing to sell (write is the term in option-speak) a board lot of contracts. Board lots in this case refers to 10 contracts.

If a stock like Nortel has a call option with an at-the-money strike valued at $170, the three-month contracts would read something like bid $10.50, ask $10.90—a spread of 40 cents, whereas the spread on the stock would typically only be a nickel or a dime. The reason for the spread is primarily because of liquidity and more specifically volume or interest in the option. The options market makers are required to keep a minimum spread such that it maintains the appearance of liquidity. As a result, what appears on the quote screen may be artificial. An exception is the last trade, which is, of course, the last price at which a trade was performed.

Given the appearance of an artificial market, sizing is very important when trading options. Another key element of the quote is open interest, a term unique to options trading and refers to the number of contracts which are still "open." A contract is open if a client bought an options contact and hadn't sold it or exercised it yet, or on the other side of the market, if a client had sold or written a contract and not bought it back yet. These happen to be the opposite sides of the same contract and make up the same open interest. Therefore if a client bought 10 Nortel January 90 call contracts, by definition there would have to be someone on the other side of the market selling 10 Nortel January 90 call contracts and thus there would be open interest of 10.

An Option Trade Done on the Phone Might Sound Like This

Client: Hello. I'd like to get a quote on Bombardier Class B, please.

Agent: What's the account number please?

Client: 12345678

Agent: OK. BBD.b bid 26.85; ask 26.90; last at 26.85; up 65 cents on 400,000 shares.

Client: Can I now get an option quote for the same?

Agent: Certainly. What strike price and expiry are you looking at?

Client: Can you give me the March 27.50 calls?*

Agent: Sure, bidding .65; asking .90; last at .60; no volume,
open interest of 35.

Client: OK. I'd like to place an order for 10 March 27.50
strikes for $.75.

Agent: So, we're buying 10 call option contracts
March 27 1/2s on Bombardier Class B.

Agent: And how long will that order be good for?

Client: Just for the day.

Agent: Are we debiting your bank account or settling in the
account here?

Client: Use the cash available in the brokerage account,
please.

Agent: Is this an opening or closing transaction?

Client: Opening.

Agent: OK. Then, confirming on the order to purchase 10 call
option contracts on Bombardier Class B March 27 1/2
calls at .75; opening transaction; good for the day;
and we're using cash in the account. Is this correct?

Client: Yes.

Agent: OK, then. Your order has been entered. Is there anything else I can help you with?

Client: No, thanks.

Agent: Thanks for calling.

---

* When interpreting the option quote, the month stated represents the month in
which the option expires. It is understood that options expire on the third Friday of
the indicated month so it is up to the individual to know exactly what day they will
expire. The 27.50 means the exercise price of the option is $27.50—so any time up to
and including the third Friday of the indicated month the option trader can exercise
her right to buy the stock for $27.50.

A Few Points for Options Traders to Consider

- Options are wasting assets, which means that they have a definite lifespan. Given their time to expiry, buying options is not for the long-term investor.

- The volatility of options can be quite impressive even compared to some of the wilder stocks out there. This is because of the implicit leverage.

- Even though American-style options enable you to trade the option any time up to and including the expiry date, you should watch them daily for price movements. Here's a true story to illustrate why. A client of one particular discount brokerage once bought 10 call option contracts on Alcan and, with the stock price unmoving for many days, he forgot to check the option on the day it expired (options technically expire on the third Friday of the month). That particular day, the stock rose significantly—enough that the option contract was worth almost $1.00. On Canadian and US options, if the option is worth $0.75 or more at expiry it is automatically exercised, meaning that he ended up buying 1,000 shares of Alcan that he really couldn't afford (10 contracts times 100 shares).

- Beware the spread—often the spread on the option quote can be prohibitively large. In some cases a $0.50 spread on Canadian options is not uncommon.

- An option strategy where you're not really sure which way a stock will go is to buy a put and a call on the same stock. Ask your broker how commissions will be charged in this case. Some will charge one commission on this transaction because both the put and the call are purchased on the same stock, whereas others charge two commissions.

- Beware the fast market—a "fast market" is declared by the exchange floor official at the request of the market maker. This is generally triggered when there is an influx of orders in an option class generally because of mirrored activity in the underlying interest. During a fast market orders are carried out by open cry.

Options Basics for Discount Clients

Options are a derivative product, which sounds impressive but just means they derive from the underlying interest (for our purposes a stock) on which they are bought and sold. There are essentially two types of options, calls and puts and they are opposites of each other. A call allows you to buy a security at a guaranteed predetermined price for up to nine months (longer ones are called LEAPs—long range equity anticipation securities) for a cost which is called the premium. A put guarantees a selling price.

Those are the technical definitions. Now that they're out of the way, we can look at options in a way you can understand. Imagine you have a car that you want to sell that is probably worth about $1,000, but you would accept any reasonable offer. It happens that a neighbour down the street likes the car so much that he wants to buy it from you immediately, but he doesn't get paid until the end of the month. So you ask him for a couple bucks to ensure that he will be able to buy the car for $1,000 when he gets the money. He gladly pays you $25 for the option to purchase the car but not the obligation. This agreement you arrange also includes a proviso that if others see the car and want to offer more for it, say $1,100, then your neighbour would still have first rights to it at the price of $1,000. If there were few offers to buy the car and the highest someone offered was $900, your neighbour would not have to exercise his option to buy it for $1,000, but you could still keep the $25. In compensation for losing the $25, your neighbour could then buy the car at the prevailing market price of $900. For his $25, then, your neighbour would be protected against the possibility the price of the car would rise while still being able to buy it for less than he originally expected.

Now, let's work in a little jargon. What we're really talking about here is a call option contract—an option that gives your neighbour the right but not the obligation to buy the car. You, the one with the car, are the option writer (seller) and your neighbour is the call option buyer (holder). The $25 he paid is called the premium. (The premium paid would actually be much more than $25.) In exchange, you are obligated to sell the car at a predetermined price, which is the strike price or exercise price.

In this example, the call option contract works by locking in the purchase price for a period of time. The options market works essentially the same way. Continuing with the car example, there would be different prices at which the buyer could lock in, say $900, $950, $1,000, $1,050, $1,100, and the price premium—the $25 payment in our example—would be based on the likelihood that the car's value would appreciate beyond the $1,000 strike price. If the car's market value was $1,000 and your neighbour bought the option to guarantee a $1,000 purchase price, then that $1,000 price is called "at the money." If he bought a contract guaranteeing to a purchase price of $950, then the contract would be "in the money"—in the money by $50 as a matter of fact (you arrive at this by taking the $1,000 market value of the car and subtracting the $950 strike price). And if the purchase price was locked in at $1,050, then the contract would be out of the money given its market value of $1,000. In the real world the price of the option is based on a number of criteria, including the underlying value of the asset, volatility, interest rates and time to expiry.

Now, let's say you had a GIC that was locked-in for three months, and you wanted to buy a stock right now because you felt there will be a significant rise in the short-term price. If you waited to buy the stock until the GIC matured, you feel the stock would cost considerably more than now. What do you do? Buy a call option contract to ensure that you can purchase the shares at the price you want.

Now you have to enter a new parameter to the equation—the length of time you can purchase the options for. Option contracts generally have a three-, six- and nine-month expiry rotation. So not only do you have a choice of price, you also have a choice of time frame. A sample of the choices available might look like this:

Figure 1: Options Choices

month of expiry	in the money strike prices		at the money strike prices	out of the money strike prices	
Jan	90	95	100	105	110
April	90	95	100	105	110
July	90	95	100	105	110

If the stock was trading at $100, obviously the 90 strikes would be worth more than the others since the option entitles you to purchase the stock at $90. Because the stock can be purchased at $100 in the market the 90 strikes would logically have a value of at least $10. But what if you could buy the 90s for $8? Then you could theoretically pay the $8 for the option, then exercise the option to buy the stock for $90 and immediately sell the stock back into the market for $100. You make $2 with no risk—not a bad investment.

The difference between the strike price and the market value of the stock is called the intrinsic value. In this case, the intrinsic value of the 90s would be $10. The 95s would have an intrinsic value of $5, while the 100s would have an intrinsic value of 0, as would the out-of-the-money strikes 105s and 110s.

Now let's consider the July strikes. They would be worth more to investors because of the likelihood of the stock appreciating in value over nine months is greater than it would be over three months. So the most expensive call option premium would be the July 90s. Conversely, the least expensive would be the Jan 110s, since they expire sooner and they entitle you to buy the stock at $110 when you can actually buy it on the market for $100 now. Why would someone ever buy the out of the money Jan 110s? It really comes down to the relationship between risk and return. If you were to buy these call options it would likely cost you very little, but if the stock did appreciate over the three months from now until January, then the returns could be fabulous.

If we look at the 90 strike price for the stock in January, April and July, we see that the intrinsic value is the same. Market value minus the strike price in all cases is the same: $10. But, we know intuitively that because the stock's price has a better chance of appreciating over nine months than it does over six months and a much better chance than it does in three months, the price for the nine-month 90 strikes would cost more than the six- or the three-month versions. This is because of time value. Time value of an option is what is left over once you subtract the strike price from the market value.

Suppose the option strike price was $100 and the premium for the call was $5. The maximum loss would be the premium paid and would exist if the stock price remained below $105. Above $105 is the profit.

What About Puts?

We've talked about calls so far but what about puts? Calls enable you to lock in a purchase price, whereas puts let you lock in a sale price. Imagine you happen to own the stock we spoke of above and that it's currently trading at $100. In doing your research, you feel the stock has potential to depreciate in value over the short term, and you don't want to sell the stock because of its long-term potential. You simply want to protect your investment just in case. One solution would be to buy a put.

Puts enable you to sell the stock for a predetermined price. So if you wanted to guarantee the sale price of $100 you would pay a premium for the right to sell the stock at that price. If the stock happens to drop over the short term, say to $95, you would still be able to sell the stock at $100. The intrinsic value of the option would be $5. If the stock traded at $100 or above until the option expired in three months, then you would lose the premium. These are often called protective puts.

Now, say a put option contract is purchased for $5 on a $100 stock. The maximum loss occurs when the stock price remains at or above $95. A profit exists below that point to a maximum of $95 (assuming stock price goes to $0).

You may be wondering if you have to hold onto the options until expiry. Most options that you'll come across are American-style, which means that you don't have to wait until it expires before you can exercise them. (European-style options restrict investors from exercising before the strike price). In the case of call options, if the stock goes up you can do one of a few things. You can exercise the option, or you can sell it in the market. If the $100 stock appreciates by $1, the at the money and in the money options would appreciate in line by $1 or very close to $1. The out of the money options would appreciate by somewhat less than a dollar. You can sell the option for a relatively large gain.

What Are the Choices for Option Trading?

Option trading is generally linked to stocks, but you can also use stock indexes, futures, bonds and currencies, although most discounters are not likely to offer these. The security that the option is tied to is called the underlying interest.

Not all stocks have options on them. In fact, while many stocks in the US market have options, few in Canada do. Even fewer have much volume. The stocks that have options on them in Canada are listed below:

Figure 2: Canadian Stocks with Options

STOCK	SYMBOL
BARRICK GOLD	ABX
AIR CANADA	AC
AGRIUM	AGU
ALCAN	AL
ANDERSON EXPL	AXL
BCE INC	BCE
BID.COM	BII
BALLARD POWER	BLD
BNS	BNS
BIOMIRA	BRA
CELESTICA	CLS

CIBC	CM
COREL	COR
CDN PACIFIC	CP
COGNOS	CSN
EURO-NEVADA	EN
GEAC	GAC
HUMMINGBIRD	HUM
IMPERIAL OIL	IMO
JDS UNIPHASE	JDU
KINROSS	K
MOORE CORP	MCL
MAGNA INTL	MG.A
MACKENZIE FIN	MKF
MITEL	MLT
INCO	N
NEWBRIDGE NET	NNC
NEWCOURT	NCT
NORTEL NETWORKS	NT
NOVA CORP	NVQ
PETRO CANADA	PCA
PRECISION DRILLING	PD
PLACER DOME	PDG
ROGERS COMMUN	RCI.B
ROYAL BANK	RY
SUNCOR ENERGY	SU
TORONTO DOM	TD
TRIMARK FIN	TMF
THOMSON CORP	TOC
TRANSCANADA PIPELINES	TRP
TVX GOLD	TVX
TRIZEC HAHN	TZH
SEAGRAM CO	VO

So far, we have looked at what happens when you buy an option. You pay a premium on the call or the put and hope the underlying stock goes up for calls and down for puts. Now, let's examine what happens on the other side of the market. When you buy an option, where do you buy it from? Although you buy the option on the market, there is another person on the other side of the market selling the contract. The Options Clearing Corporation acts as an intermediary.

Let's say you own a $100 stock and the call options have the same strike prices as mentioned earlier. You sell the option and receive the premium that the call option buyer pays. What benefit do you derive from doing this? If you expect the stock's value to drop or remain the same over the short period you can sell the option and receive the premium to increase your returns. So if the stock remains in the same price range in the three months until the option expires, you keep the premium. But in the same vein, if the underlying stock value increases, the option buyer still has the right to buy the stock at the strike price, and you would be obligated to deliver it to him or her. The downside would be that you'd have to deliver the shares at the strike price. This procedure is called covered writing or selling.

Can you write a contract without owning the underlying stock? Yes, but watch out. This process is similar to the above scenario where you receive the premium for writing the contract, but you don't actually own the stock. You can benefit from writing the contract again if the underlying stock remains in the same range or drops. Danger prevails when the stock increases and you are required to deliver. You would have to deliver the shares at the predetermined strike price and you might have to buy them in the market for considerably more than you expected. This is called naked call option writing.

Now, let's examine what happens when you sell the option on a put option contract. Say you own the stock and expect it to rise in value. You would like to earn income off your investment in the underlying stock, so you decide to sell a put option contract. The put option buyer has the right to sell the stock and, as the writer of the contract, you would agree to purchase the shares at the pre-arranged strike price if the stock drops. However, if the stock remains neutral or increases in value, the option premium remains yours.

Many discount brokers do not allow clients to write naked option contracts because of the unlimited risk potential, although exceptions may be made for truly experienced, knowledgeable and well-heeled investors.

Basic Option Trading Strategy: Buy Calls and Invest the Difference

Let's say you thought that BCE shares were going to appreciate in value in the six months from January to July. An idea would be to buy a BCE call option with July expiry that would enable you to buy the underlying BCE common for the amount indicated in the contract, the strike price.

If BCE were trading at $165 and you didn't wish to put up the whole amount for the trade today, you could buy the call option for a premium, which would likely be around $5.00 per contract (a contract represents 100 shares of the underlying security). So for $500 plus the commission paid to the broker, you could guarantee the future purchase price of $165 for the BCE shares. In the meantime, you're free to invest in money market instruments or anything else to offset the premium charged.

The purpose of this strategy is to take advantage of the potential increased value of the security. If by the time the option contract is set to expire the BCE shares trade at $170, you would have benefitted from this strategy by being able to buy BCE at $165 regardless of its market price.

A caveat is that there are generally no restrictions on when you sell your options. If BCE quickly increased in value to $170 a share you could unload your contracts and make a profit off selling the options into the market because the purchaser would then be able to buy BCE shares for $65 even though they now trade at $170. The option value would have increased similar to the common shares. If the common shares increased $5, the option would likely have increased by at least $5 and, therefore, had you paid $500 for the one contract, you may be able to sell it for $10/contract or $1,000, essentially doubling your money. Alternatively, you could exercise the options and acquire the BCE shares at $165 even though they now trade on the market for $170.

In this example, you bought a contract that enabled you to buy the underlying BCE shares for the same price six months forward as they were currently trading. These options are called at the money. Had you bought a contract, for a reduced premium, to purchase Bell shares at $170 instead of $165, these options are said to be out of the money. It may have cost you only $2/contract or $200 instead of $500, but the potential losses are greater when a option trades out of the money. Still, if you wished to buy a contact that allowed you to buy the underlying shares at less than what where it currently trades, then these contracts are said to trade in the money.

Options are similar to buying on leverage in that the gains or losses are accentuated by the movements in the underlying common shares. In the first case, a $5 move in the stock reflected a 100 per cent move on the option. If the option was out of the money and allowed you to buy the shares at $170 within six months and the stock experienced a $5 move, the $200 contract may now be worth almost $500 or an increase of 150 per cent. The in the money contract which allowed you to buy BCE at $160 for a premium of, say, $11 would increase to $16, a safer investment but only a 45 per cent increase.

Combinations

If you expect the share price of the underlying security to move dramatically in one way or another depending on, for example, its earnings, to benefit from the movement with little exposure to risk you may want to buy a combination. In other words, you'd buy a call and a put on the same stock. If the stock goes up dramatically you benefit from the surge, and if the stock goes down you'd benefit from the fall. (You must factor in the premiums and commissions, though.)

A specific type of option strategy called a straddle involves buying a call and a put on the same stock in hopes that its price will move dramatically either up or down. A straddle is very specific in that it involves the purchase of the same number of call and put option contracts with the same strike price and same expiry.

Some discounters will allow for straddles and other sophisticated options trading strategies, however, not all do. Some will charge just one commission to enter a straddle, whereas others will charge two—one for each side of the transaction.

Web Resources for Options Traders

www.cboe.com: The Chicago Board Options Exchange, the world's top options exchange, has an educational section that makes options as understandable as they'll ever be. It also includes descriptions of the many option products traded.

www.coveredcalls.com: This free newsletter also includes covered call options rankings.

www.futuresource.com: This is a sort of supersite for options traders, with quotes, charts, news and more. It's focused on US markets.

www.optionscentral.com: This educational site offers free software, videos and seminars in the United States as well as Canada. It is run by the Options Industry Council.

www.optionclub.com: The Option Club includes analysis of option strategies, plus links to other investing Web sites for news and quotes. They bill themselves as "the premier option research site for option investors and traders."

10

Bells and Whistles

The phrase discount broker is a little outdated and even misleading because it calls to mind a service that offers little more than cheap prices. If you had to pick an analogy, it would be the kind of store where the goods go for less and the only service available is at the checkout counter. Discounters used to be that way, but the business is far too competitive today for anyone to get away with providing nothing more than cheap trade execution. At a bare minimum, a good discounter will offer a range of features that will help keep you in touch with the markets and help you do your own research on stocks and mutual funds. Beyond these features are such services as dividend reinvestment plans (DRIPs), seminars on investing topics and trading in languages besides English and French.

Extras Offered

Let's take a look at some of the extras that discount brokers offer, starting with those meant to help clients keep up with the markets and research stocks, bonds and mutual funds.

Market Updates

This is a basic extra that everybody does differently. Ideally, you'd get continuously updated levels for stocks, bonds and currencies and the ability to zero in on a particular market to track hot stocks. Some discounter Web sites allow you to customize a home page to show selected market indices and stock quotes.

Real-Time Quotes and Charts

Unless you subscribe to an on-line market information service, most of the stock and market quotes you'll find on the Web will be delayed by 15 or 20 minutes. In fast-moving markets, that's next to useless. Real-time quotes reflect the latest trading developments on a stock and are thus much more useful in deciding the right price to bid or ask for a stock.

Be warned that some brokers only give you real-time quotes on the Internet when you're placing a trade. If you're just calling up a quick quote out of curiosity, you get delayed data. Another approach is to give investors a set number of free real-time quotes, then charge for any used above that. For instance, E*Trade Canada gives you 50 free real-time quotes for equities and options each month and then charges at a rate of 15 cents per quote. Place a successful trade and you receive an additional 300 free quotes. E*Trade also offers unlimited quotes with a 20-minute time delay.

Many discounters give you the means to graph a stock's recent price trend. If you plan to use this feature, make sure your broker's Web site allows you some flexibility in deciding what exactly you're going to graph. For example, do you just get a simple one-year price graph marked off in weekly increments, or can you adjust the timelines, add moving averages and comparisons against other stocks or indexes?

News

Many brokers give you access to both general daily market news and stories related to specific companies. Generally, you type in the symbol of a stock you're following and a list of recent documents comes up. Some may be from financial news services such as Reuters, Dow Jones and Bloomberg, while others might be from news release services like Canada NewsWire. Be sure you know the difference. A news service will give you an objective summary of what a company has announced, while news release services carry press releases written or approved by the company itself.

Equity Research

Discounter brokers can't recommend investments, but they can provide you with the tools needed to make your own decisions. There are really two kinds of research available from discounters. The first, which we'll call fundamental information, is the most common. Generally, you select a company or mutual fund and request a faxed or on-line report that lays out financials, ratios, recent corporate developments and so on. Generally, the reports come from third-party suppliers such as Standard & Poor's, MPL Communications or Argus. The intended audience would be investors who know their ratios and are comfortable going through financial statements. If you know how to interpret these numbers, research that provides background information can be extremely useful.

Some brokers offer such reports for free, while others charge for them on a pay-as-you go basis that usually includes discounts for clients who buy in bulk. At TD Waterhouse, for example, research is priced in units that cost $3.50 each or less if you buy units in bulk (66 units would cost $2.50 each).

The second, much more precious kind of research is an opinionated report by an analyst on a particular company, complete with a buy/sell recommendation. CT Securities became the first to offer this service to clients in fall 1999 when it put a small collection of reports on its trading Web site and offered clients free access. The reports were written by analysts working for CT's institutional arm. TD Waterhouse was close behind, offering a much larger number of reports by TD Securities analysts to clients at a small cost.

There's actually a third research category, but it's hardly worth mentioning. In an effort to pad out their no-cost research offerings, some brokers will provide a list of links to other investing

Web sites that you've probably already come across on your own. Links are nice and all, but what you really want from your broker's research menu are things you can't get yourself.

Here's a rundown of the equity research offered by all the discount brokers. Remember to check your broker's Web site for the most up-to-date offerings.

Bank of Montreal InvestorLine

Free Stuff: Bank of Montreal economics reports; a link to the research tool Carlson On-line.

You pay for: Carlson's deluxe service at a 20-per-cent discount (includes a screening tool for companies on all major Canadian exchanges, financial data and insider trading information and short positions).

Overall rating: InvestorLine has plans to improve the research and new services available to clients.

Charles Schwab Canada

Free Stuff: Fundamental research by Zacks on over 2,200 Canadian companies, including 700 with analyst recommendation summaries; market and economic commentary and recommendation lists by Pershing Investment Research, a division of Donaldson, Lufkin and Jenrette; Financial Post Corporate Profiler reports on 4,500 Canadian companies; access to Bloomberg financial data; on-line analyst centre for researching stocks.

You pay for: Additional third-party research.

Overall rating: Excellent. Great variety.

CIBC Investor's Edge

Free Stuff: On-line access to Zacks reports on more than 2,000 Canadian and 8,000 US companies, including earnings estimates and analyst recommendations; an on-line stock-screening service; reports from CIBC's economics department.

You pay for: Check with Investor's Edge.

Overall rating: Much improved. Check in for the latest developments.

CT Securities

Free Stuff: On-line access to reports and comments by CT's in-house analysts on roughly 30 different companies and economic sectors, including buy/sell recommendations; research reports on about 50 mutual funds recommended by CT analysts; links to equity and mutual fund Web sites; in-house market commentary.

You pay for: Automated phone access to third-party equity research reports either individually or in packages.

Overall rating: Good. Not much breadth, but lots of it is free.

Disnat

Free Stuff: A monthly newsletter called Focus Research is sent with your monthly account statement each month. This publication, written by analysts at sister company Desjardins Securities, covers major Canadian and global economic and financial market developments and offers both analysis and recommendations on the shares of Quebec-based companies.

You pay for: Nothing.

Overall rating: Incomplete. Not really in the game as far as do-it-yourself research tools go.

E*Trade Canada

Free Stuff: Interactive charting from BigCharts, US market analysis from briefing.com, US company profiles from Baseline Financial Services, Canadian and US earnings estimates and company profiles from Zacks, exhaustive links to investing Web sites in Canada and abroad.

You pay for: Research reports and recommendations from York-ton Securities, an investment dealer specializing in the technology area. Costs $15 per month.

Overall rating: Good. Lots to keep you busy.

HSBC InvestDirect

Free stuff: Free access to Zacks research, free monthly economic and investing reports by HSBC and Argus a stock-screening tool and access to more than 20 newswires from around the world.

You pay for: Corporate reports by Standard & Poor's, First Call, Vickers and MPL; S&P Marketscope (market commentary); S&P stock screens. Discounts available on InTechTra Hong Kong Stock report and Carlson On-line.

Overall rating: Very good. Nice variety.

National Bank Discount Brokerage

Free stuff: Detailed on-line market summaries updated at 9 a.m. and again at 12 p.m.

You pay for: Nothing.

Overall rating: Watch for improvements.

Royal Bank Action Direct

Free Stuff: Financial Post Corporate Profiler offers financial and other data on 4,500 Canadian public companies; more detailed Financial Post Corporate Reports focus in on 500 Canadian firms; extensive links to other investing Web sites.

You pay for: First Call earnings reports, Standard & Poor's stock reports, Financial Post Investor summaries (include analyst buy/sell recommendations).

Overall rating: Quite good. The Financial Post profiles are amazingly detailed.

Scotia Discount Brokerage

Free stuff: News releases.

You pay for: Nothing.

Overall rating: Poor but then Scotia Discount's pitch is low commissions, not client amenties.

Sun Life Securities

Free stuff: Just charts, quotes and news/features.

You pay for: Nothing.

Overall rating: Poor. Sun Life is still a new service, so look for improvements over time.

TD Waterhouse

Free Stuff: Free access to the US Web site Briefing.com, which provides fast daily market commentary; Zacks profiles of 8,000 US and Canadian companies, including analyst buy/sell recommendations and financial data; a stock-screening tool that permits searches according to 15 different criteria.

You pay for: Reports and e-mail morning updates on Canadian and US companies by TD Securities analysts, complete with buy/sell recommendations; S&P Marketscope, a financial news and commentary service; stock reports from Standard & Poor's, First Call, Vickers and MPL; a stock-screening tool from S&P.

Overall rating: Quite possibly the best out there.

Mutual Fund Research

This area deserves special mention because just about all discounters are courting fund investors with good, free research tools you use over the Internet. In many cases, you don't even have to be a client to use them. The only word of warning is that quality varies widely, so be sure to take a test drive if this feature is important to you.

The better fund research tools—TD Waterhouse and E*Trade Canada come to mind—come reasonably close to some of the professional fund research software available. Generally, they're more than up to the job of helping you winnow a list of funds down to a few choice picks. Let's say you were looking for a Canadian equity fund for your RRSP portfolio, something with a long-term track record of decent returns and a low MER. With a fund research tool, you could punch up a list of funds that have an annual average compound return of 10 per cent over 10 years and an MER of under 2 per cent.

Feeling risk-averse? Some tools will let you sort as well by standard deviation, a measure of how volatile a security is. Once you had the list, you could call up individual profiles of each of the funds. You might find, for example, that some funds are too heavily weighted in a particular sector for your taste or that a long-time manager has moved on and been replaced by what appears to be a fresh-faced rookie—good reasons to take a pass and look elsewhere.

The more sophisticated fund research tools will let you look up opinions on funds from the authors of some of the more prominent fund rating books. Others, notably TD Waterhouse, will let you do head-to-head comparison charts or compile lists of funds that excel in particular areas and then combine them into one master list.

Here's a rundown of the mutual fund research offered by all the discount brokers. Remember to check broker Web sites for the latest offerings.

Bank of Montreal InvestorLine

Free Stuff: FundFinder is an on-line tool that lets users search for funds according to various criteria and provides bare-bones fund profiles.

You Pay For: Nothing.

Overall rating: OK, but not as good as some.

Charles Schwab Canada

Free Stuff: Fund analysis is available through the Schwab trading desk.

You Pay For: Nothing.

Overall rating: An on-line fund research tool would be nice.

CIBC Investor's Edge

Free Stuff: Through the Investor's Edge Mutual Fund Market, clients have on-line access to research on funds and fund companies, as well as tools for sorting, comparing and charting funds.

You Pay For: Nothing.

Overall rating: A good range of services.

CT Securities

Free Stuff: The Mutual Fund Select List, is a compilation of 50-odd funds in all major sectors that have been recommended by CT analysts along with short reports on each.

You Pay For: Nothing.

Overall rating: Good. The recommended list is a useful resource.

Disnat

Free Stuff: Disnat's Mutual Fund Selection Service allows you to choose and analyze funds and can be accessed on-line or by telephone.

You Pay For: Nothing.

Overall rating: Not bad.

E*Trade Canada

Free Stuff: Screening and graphing tools that give you the ability to do head-to-head fund comparisons, fund profiles with information such as Top 10 holdings, ratings by fund analysts and monthly commentaries from Gordon Pape.

You Pay For: Nothing.

Overall rating: Excellent.

HSBC InvestDirect

Free stuff: Fund Strategist is a monthly report that includes investing and asset allocation tips, and it also has fund picks by the Fund Counsel publication.

You pay for: Additional mutual fund reports.

Overall rating: Good.

National Bank Discount Brokerage

Free stuff: Commentaries and information reports can be either faxed or mailed, along with recommendations from in-house analysts.

You pay for: Nothing.

Overall rating: Good.

Royal Bank Action Direct

Free stuff: Fund Analyzer lets you screen and graph funds online, then call up detailed profiles.

You pay for: Nothing.

Overall rating: Very good.

Scotia Discount Brokerage

Free stuff: An on-line fund research tool allows limited fund screening but provides detailed profiles.

You pay for: Nothing.

Overall rating: OK, but not the best-looking fund research tool around.

Sun Life Securities

Free stuff: None.

You pay for: Nothing.

Overall rating: Not a contender in this area, but stand by.

TD Waterhouse

Free stuff: One of the most technically advanced on-line fund-screening tools offered by a Canadian discounter, plus detailed fund profiles; Analysts' Choice funds selected by TD Asset Management analysts, fund profiles.

You pay for: Additional fund analysis software.

Overall rating: Top notch.

Don't Miss These Free Bonuses For Discount Broker Clients

Bank of Montreal InvestorLine: AccountLink turns your brokerage account in into a bank account with no monthly fee—a huge bonus for InvestorLine clients.

Charles Schwab Canada: The top-notch on-line research centre. You can find your own numbers to crunch or look at analyst consensus recommendations and earnings estimates.

CIBC Investor's Edge: News reports. Type in a stock symbol and you receive all recent material from Canadian Corporate News, Reuters and Dow Jones On-line News (which includes the *Wall Street Journal*).

CT Securities: Free analyst reports. Researching your own stocks is fine, but a second opinion from professional analysts can be welcome.

Disnat: The Focus Research newsletter comes each month with your account statement and includes stock recommendations as well as economic and financial market analysis.

E*Trade Canada: The research area on E*Trade's Web site has a great collection of tools for do-it-yourself investors.

HSBC InvestDirect: Free economic and investment research reports from HSBC and Argus.

National Bank Discount Brokerage: The mutual fund advisory service will help you choose a fund and fax or mail you commentary by their own analysts at no cost.

Royal Bank Action Direct: Free access to Financial Post Corporate Reports and Corporate Filer, an exhaustive source of data about thousands of public companies.

Scotia Discount Brokerage: Receive a stock alert on your Scotia home page when a stock you're watching reaches a price set by you.

Sun Life Securities: The best bonus here is Sun points. You get 100 Sun points every month for keeping your account with Sun Life and 100 every time you do a transaction. The points can be used to purchase real-time quotes, charts and news. One real-time quote goes for a point, news goes for two points and a chart costs three.

TD Waterhouse: Research nobody offers more.

Newsletters

Mostly, you'll find bland platitudes in these monthly account statement throw-ins. "Bonds...essential for every portfolio," one headline blared recently in TD Waterhouse's very sharp-looking newsletter. But don't just toss your newsletter out. Often, this is the place you'll learn about new services or commission changes at your broker. You may also come across the odd article of interest, especially in those cases where outside investment writers, money managers and economists have been invited to contribute an article.

If you want to subscribe to a particular outside investing newsletter or on-line service, your discount broker may well be able to get you a discount. Ask for an up-to-date list of what's available.

With all the focus on stock-trading, discounters sometimes don't get around to clearly explaining all the client benefits they have to offer. Here, we've rounded up some notable services that you may not be aware of.

Initial Public Offerings (IPOs)

The ability for an investor to get in on "the ground floor" of an IPO for a new public company is often viewed as a big advantage. Some recent US tech stock IPOs have fostered the idea that getting in on a new stock issue is a surefire way to make money. It isn't necessarily. Many IPOs in Canada have turned out badly, with Eaton's being only one example.

In the past, discount brokerage clients have been at a disadvantage when it comes to gaining access to IPOs. Shares tended to be allocated to the big full-service brokerages, which often underwrote the issue, and their clients were the ones to benefit. These days, discounters are getting into the game a little more than they used to. Charles Schwab Canada has introduced an on-line public offering Web site—**www.canada ipo.com**—that allows clients to view the prospectus for a new stock issue, as well as see a marketing presentation by the issuer of the stock and express an interest in buying the new issue.

E*Trade Canada has struck a deal that allows it to distribute new issues underwritten by Yorkton Securities, a smaller dealer with a high-tech specialty. TD Waterhouse plays up its IPO capability by offering a quicklink on its Web site home page to a list of new issues. As well, TD clients can register for e-mail notification of upcoming new issues.

Most other discounters list IPOs among their product offerings, but they don't make a big deal about it. If you're interested in IPOs, ask your discounter what's available. Remember, though, that the hottest new issues will still go to the full-service brokers and their clients with little left over for the discount crowd. Remember, also, that you're not missing much since most Canadian IPOs end up trading lower than their issue price very quickly.

If you're interested in a new issue, you have to first review the preliminary prospectus, then indicate the maximum number of shares you want to buy and the maximum price you're willing to pay (you will be provided with an estimated pricing range). When the final prospectus is issued, you'll be contacted providing the final pricing is within your limit. You can cancel the order any time up until a receipt has been issued for the final prospectus. By the way, although new equity issues tend to get most of the attention, the term IPOs also applies to bonds.

Dividend Reinvestment Plans (DRIPs)

DRIPs let existing shareholders of certain companies buy additional shares without incurring brokerage commissions. The idea is to use the dividends paid by the shares to purchase more stock. There are two ways to enrol in a DRIP. The first is to buy shares in a particular company from a broker, then have them registered and delivered to you (see below for a description of how to do this). The next step is to call the investor relations department at the company in question and ask for a DRIP enrolment form. Complete the form and send it back to the company or to the trust company acting as transfer agent for the DRIP.

The second way to set up a DRIP is to request in writing that your discount broker take your quarterly dividends and reinvest them in new shares. This method sounds simple, but there are a couple of drawbacks. While the usual buy commissions aren't applied to broker DRIPs, there are often administrative fees. As well, most brokers won't allow you to buy fractional shares.

Company DRIPS often let you do this, which is a real plus because you can put all of your dividends back to work.

Here's an example to show the benefits of a discounter-run DRIP. Let's say you hold 1,000 shares of fictional company, Widgetco. The annual dividend of $1.20, paid in quarterly installments of 30 cents, is to go directly toward the purchase of more company shares. If Widgetco shares trade at $20 each, the $300 quarterly dividend will buy 15 additional shares. The same thing will happen in the next quarter, except the 30-cent dividend will be paid on 1,015 shares, not 1,000. The extra 15 shares would only generate $4.50 worth of dividends, which is not enough to buy another full share. That money would remain in cash.

If you want to set up a broker DRIP, be sure to ask which stocks are available because the number varies widely. Another question is whether a DRIP stock can be a held within your regular investing account or whether you need a separate account for the DRIP.

Figure 1: Discounter DRIPs and Associated Costs

Broker	Charge
Bank of Montreal InvestorLine	None
Charles Schwab	Initial $10/stock + $2.50/dividend
CIBC Investor's Edge	$1/dividend Canada & US stocks*
CT Securities	None
Disnat	No DRIPs offered
E*Trade Canada	No DRIPs offered
HSBC InvestDirect	None
National Bank Discount Brokerage	None
Royal Bank Action Direct	None
Scotia Discount Brokerage	None
Sun Life Securities	Initial $10/stock + $2.50/dividend
TD Waterhouse	$1/dividend
* Most brokers that offer DRIPs do so on both Cdn and US stocks.	

DRIP-Related Web Sites

www.cibcmellon.com/drips: CIBC Mellon Trust Company is one of the largest transfer agents for Canadian companies. Its Web site is full of information on DRIPs.

www.montrealtrust.com: Montreal Trust is another large transfer agent. Its Web site lays out information on DRIPs and the programs available, including a DRIP calculator.

www.ndir.com/stocks.drips.html: The Directions Web site includes a list of DRIP companies, as well as information on the costs of setting up a DRIP at the various discount brokers.

www.canadianmoneysaver.ca/reg_drip.htm: This monthly investing magazine's Web site contains a fabulous primer on how company DRIPs and broker DRIPs work.

Foreign Markets

Every discount broker offers access to all of Canada's stock markets—the Toronto Stock Exchange, the Montreal Exchange and the Canadian Venture Exchange. As well, everyone offers access to the New York Stock Exchange, the American Stock Exchange and its sister operation, Nasdaq, home to the hottest technology stocks. When it comes to foreign markets, though, there are a lot of differences between brokers. (US markets are not considered foreign.)

Foreign market access might not sound all that important, given that there are thousands of North American stocks to choose from, not to mention a wide selection of foreign stocks that trade on the New York Stock Exchange. Besides, exposure to foreign markets is easily obtained through a global equity mutual fund or index-based investments like World Equity Benchmarks (WEBs), which mirror the performances of stock markets in 17 countries around the world and are sold on the American Stock Exchange. This may be fine for the average investor, but there are many people in Canada who came from other countries and are quite comfortable investing overseas. HSBC InvestDirect, one of the smaller discounters in Canada, has carved out a profitable niche catering to Hong Kong émigrés who want to trade internationally.

Figure 2: Access to Foreign Markets

Bank of Montreal InvestorLine	Yes—Notably Hong Kong, London, Tokyo)
Charles Schwab	Yes–All major markets
CIBC Investor's Edge	Yes–All major markets
CT Securities	Yes—Most foreign markets;
Disnat (Caisse Desjardins)	No
E*Trade Canada	No—But coming soon
HSBC InvestDirect	Yes—Hong Kong, UK and Europe, Australia, China (Shen Zhen & Shanghai), Japan, Thailand, Singapore (Jardine & local market), Indonesia, Philippines and Malaysia
National Bank Discount Brokerage	Limited access—by special request only
Royal Bank Action Direct	No
Scotia Discount Brokerage	No
Sun Life Brokerage	No
TD Waterhouse	Yes—All major markets

Accommodation Trades

Say you have shares that you bought through a share purchase program at a company you used to work for. You want to sell these shares, but you don't have a brokerage account. It's not essential to open an account in this case. Instead, go to the bank that you deal with on a day-to-day basis. They will receive the shares on your behalf and have them sold for you. The downside is that you can't pick a selling price—you get the market price at the time the shares are sold.

Languages

English is the default language in most regions other than Quebec, although brokers generally offer the option of speaking to a trader in English or French. Some brokers also offer services in Cantonese and Mandarin. Here's a rundown of the languages in which each discounter will serve you.

Figure 3: Languages Offered by Discounters

Bank of Montreal InvestorLine: English, French, Cantonese, Mandarin

Charles Schwab: English, French, Cantonese, Mandarin

CIBC Investor's Edge: English, French, Cantonese, Mandarin

CT Securities: English, French

Disnat: French, English

E*Trade Canada: English, French

HSBC InvestDirect: English, French, Cantonese, Mandarin

National Bank Discount Broker: French, English

Royal Bank Action Direct: English, French, Cantonese, Mandarin

Scotia Discount Brokerage: English, French (in Quebec)

Sun Life Securities: English, French

TD Waterhouse: English, French, Cantonese, Mandarin

Banking Privileges

Special mention has to be made of Bank of Montreal Investor-Line's AccountLink Service because it's such a good idea. AccountLink allows you to use your brokerage account like a bank account without any service fees. You can write cheques, gain access to your account through a bank machine and make debit card purchases through Interac direct payment terminals. There's also overdraft protection available. AccountLink is pretty much a carbon copy of the cash management accounts offered by full-service brokers at costs that can range as high as $150 to $200 per year.

Some other discounters offer chequing privileges and bank machine access in a piecemeal way. Bank machine access is particularly useful because it allows you to deposit to a trading account to cover a trade or withdraw funds upon the settlement of the sale of securities.

Share Ownership and Certificate Registration Fees

There are basically two ways that you can own shares: By taking delivery of the share certificates and putting them in a safe place or by having them held electronically by the broker in what's known as street form. Street form is by far the safest and most convenient method of holding shares because of the security measures discounters use to ensure the accuracy of account holdings.

First, discounters tape their telephone calls. The taped calls ensure that should there be a discrepancy between what the client says and what the trader says, there will always be a way of settling the dispute. After the shares are purchased, the discounter is required to issue a written confirmation notice of the trade. Monthly statements offer a third method for ensuring your account is correct.

If you decide to have your shares issued in your name and then delivered to you, expect to be charged an administration fee to cover the costs involved. The fees range between $25 and $50 per registration. Some brokers will charge only a minimal fee if you want to register more shares of the same company.

Registering Shares in Your Broker's Name

Many discount clients have share certificates at home that they don't know what to do with. If you want the shares added to your account, go to one of your broker's branch offices and deliver the certificates. You'll then have to sign the back exactly the way it appears on the front of the certificate. Be ready to show identification.

The shares are then validated by the issuing corporation's transfer agent, which usually takes a few days for Canadian stocks. The shares are then put into your account and are available to be sold. For US stocks, this process can take up to 30 days.

Alerts

A few discounters offer to tip you off if a stock you're following hits a specified price level. Scotia Discount Brokerage will flash a beacon on your computer screen, but you'll only see it once you log into Scotia's Web site. At Charles Schwab Canada, they'll flash stock alerts on the display screen of a Bell Mobility PCS phone. HSBC InvestDirect will send an alert via e-mail, Bell Mobility PCS phone and Pagenet pager. At TD Waterhouse, they use a new generation of wireless phones equipped with Web browers to deliver real-time quotes. Coming features for this service include actual trading and stock alerts.

Seminars

Holding a free seminar is a tried and true method for discounters to drum up new clients and to firm up their relationship with existing clients. If you're interested, check discounter Web sites for information on seminar times, locations and topics. Some recent seminar subjects chosen at random were: CT Securities' how to pick a mutual fund like a pro, Action Direct's basics of on-line trading and TD Waterhouse's strategies for maximizing RRSP returns.

E*Trade Canada offers live Web seminars at **www.canada. etradelive.com** and plans to introduce live chats with fund managers and industry professionals. Past seminars are archived so you can watch them any time.

Giveaways, Cash and Other Promotional Stuff

Of course, you'd never base your decision on which broker to use by the special deals offered to new clients. Still, a nice little promotion involving free trades or cash payments can be tempting.

The most recent RRSP season provided a good illustration of how competition in the discount broker business is causing the various players to use promotions like these. E*Trade Canada offered five free trades (a value of $135, based on the $27 minimum stock commission), Bank of Montreal InvestorLine offered $200 to be put toward trades or account transfer costs and Royal Bank Action offered new account applicants $100 worth of free trades plus a free copy of a Royal Bank publication called *Principles of Equity Investing*. TD Waterhouse took a different tack by offering new account applicants free access to its extensive stock and mutual fund research library.

Where promotions are concerned, the best advice is to pick a good broker and then see if they have any promotions going on. Check the Web site for news of any deals, but be sure to ask the customer service people as well.

11

On-Line Learning and Research

Can somebody explain how people managed their investments before the Internet and the World Wide Web came along? How did they keep track of what the markets were doing throughout the day? How did they research companies and mutual funds that interested them? How did they find definitions of terms and jargon they didn't understand? Whatever they did, it's thankfully in the past. Today, the answers to most investing questions are instantly available at any time to anyone who has a computer with Internet access. Years ago, only a full-service broker would have access to this kind of data.

Of course, you have to know where to go to find the information you need. There are thousands of investing Web sites out there and only a minority can do something useful for you. In this chapter of the book, we'll show you the best Web sites for doing a variety of investing functions including researching a stock, screening stocks to find the ones that meet your criteria and learning more about on-line trading. We strongly lean toward free on-line investing services but have also included some fee-based ones as well. Some sites offer freebies but charge for their best material. We apologize in advance if any of the sites we provide are no longer in operation. An effort was made to pick substantial Web sites with track records, but inevitably sites will come and go.

How to Research a Stock on the Web

If you're researching US or Canadian stocks listed on US exchanges, then there are enough resources available on the Web to keep you busy for days. On the other hand, if you're interested in stocks listed only on Canadians exchanges then there's a lot less to work with. The good news is that there are an increasing number of Canadian investing sites appearing these days, and that there are several US sites with databases on Canadian stocks.

To give you an idea of how full the range of Web resources for researching stocks is, we decided to do a little investigation on Nortel Networks. It's a Canadian company, of course, but it's listed on the New York Stock Exchange as well as the Toronto Stock Exchange, and it's covered by many US analysts.

Nine Typical Questions

Now, let's see. What can we find out on the Web about Nortel? To help organize our search, let's look at nine different topics:

1. What exactly does Nortel do?
2. What news releases has the company issued recently?
3. What news reports have there been lately on the company?
4. What do analysts think about Nortel?
5. What regulatory filings has Nortel made lately?
6. What do investors think?
7. What's the financial picture like at Nortel?
8. What have Nortel shares done lately?
9. What's the insider trading and short-selling news on Nortel?

1. What exactly does Nortel do?
The best place to get the lowdown on a company is to read its annual report. The **Quicken.ca** Web site contains a link to a service that will send you free annual reports from roughly 1,900

companies listed on Canadian and US Exchanges. Unfortunately, Nortel is not among the companies included in this service. However, the report is available for downloading on the Nortel Web site—**www.nortelnetworks.com**—and you can also order an investor kit on the company. A site to check for free annual reports of US companies is called the **Public Register's Annual Report Service**. An oddball feature of the PRARS site is that users are asked to fill out surveys on their favourite brokers and favourite stocks. The results are then displayed on the site.

For phone numbers on how to contact a company and a list of the stock exchanges where its stock trades, try the company profiles on **SEDAR** (System for Electronic Document Analysis and Retreival) Web site.

---

www.quicken.ca

www.prars.com

www.sedar.com

---

2. What news releases has the company issued recently?
The latest press releases from Nortel are available on the free section of the **Carlson Online** site. **Globeinvestor** also has large archive of corporate news releases. A search for Nortel turned up 661 hits, including some recent *Globe and Mail* articles.

---

www.carlsononline.com

www.globeinvestor.com

---

3. What news reports have there been lately on the company?
Ten stories on Nortel came up in a search of stories run by the *Globe and Mail's Report on Business* over the previous seven days. The *National Post* database turned up 124 hits on Nortel in the *Financial Post* section of the newspaper. As well, the five most recent *Dow Jones* newswire stories on Nortel are available on the **dowjones.com** Web site by doing a search with the keyword Nortel. You also get the five most recent news releases and

the five most relevant Web sites. There's also a link to the five most recent *Wall Street Journal* articles on Nortel, but you have to be a paid subscriber to get those. You can also check whether Nortel has come up in the day's news by looking at the news sections of the **Reuters** and **Bloomberg** Web sites. If you want to cast the widest net possible, you could also search the **CNN** and **CBS** sites as well.

---

www.globeandmail.com

www.nationalpost.com

www.dowjones.com

www.reuters.com

www.bloomberg.com

www.cnnfn.com

cbs.marketwatch.com

---

4. What do analysts think about Nortel?

According to **Zacks**, a very popular and very good US stock research site, 26 brokers rate the stock a strong buy or buy and three rate it a hold. Their consensus earnings-per-share estimate for the next two years was US$1.08 and US$1.32 respectively. Want to read what these analysts have to say in more detail? Zacks offers free one-paragraph summaries of their reports, and it also sells the complete version.

Zacks has been building up a Canadian database and while it's limited so far, it's still well worth looking at. A quick and easy way to do this is to go to a Canadian site called **Investcom** and click on the TSE company search option. Next, click on the appropriate TSE subgroup. All constituent companies are listed there, most with a link to a Zacks analyst recommendation summary. The Nortel information obtained through this route was the same as was found directly from Zacks itself.

A slightly different view of how analysts view Nortel came from the analyst research section of **Quicken.com**'s investing page. Quicken.com includes research reports by **Multex Investor**, one of which says a poll of 25 analysts produced a consensus rating of buy/hold. Some of the most recent analyst announcements about Nortel were listed in chronological order on **411 Stocks**.

To see whether any analysts have adjusted their ratings on Nortel during the course of the trading day, check **CNET Investor's** broker reports page. Nortel didn't come up, but if it had you could have clicked on a link and seen all the analyst announcements regarding the company dating back several months.

Wright Investors' Service, which provides free reports on a wide variety of companies, gives Nortel a top A rating in investment acceptance and an excellent B rating in financial strength and profitability/stability. Wright reports also include a detailed share price analysis and a corporate overview. Another site with free reports is **FinancialWeb**. Its Nortel report is from a firm called VectorVest and it rates the company a buy.

---

www.zacks.com

www.investcom.com

www.quicken.com

www.multex.com

www.411stocks.com

www.cnetinvestor.com

www.wisi.com

www.financialweb.com

---

5. What regulatory filings has Nortel made lately?
All regulatory filings by Canadian companies are easily available on the **SEDAR** Web site. You can search by type of document under a particular company name or for all documents filed by that company. You can then download the document using Adobe Acrobat software. Nortel's most recent annual report, audited annual financial results and management proxy/information circular were all available for download on SEDAR in English and in French. All told, there were several screens' worth of documents going back to January 1997. Carlson Online's free service includes a link to the SEDAR page for whatever company you're investigating

For Nortel's filings to the US Securities and Exchange Commission, try **MoneyCentral** or **Quicken.com**. Neither of them had anything available for Nortel when checked. However, there were several Nortel filings available on the Web site for the US Securities Exchange Commission's **EDGAR** (Electronic Data Gathering, Analysis, and Retrieval) Web site. Documents appear on the EDGAR site 24 hours after they have been filed. Another site for searching the Edgar Database is called **FreeEDGAR**.

---

www.sedar.com
www.carlsononline.com
moneycentral.msn.com
www.quicken.com
www.sec.gov/edgarhp.htm
www.freeedgar.com

---

6. *What do investors think?*

Raging Bull had 3,974 postings on its message boards about Nortel, while **Silicon Investor**, a site renowned for its high-tech message boards, had 3,860 postings on the company. Sample topics include recent analyst recommendations on Nortel, the company's position in relation to competitors like Lucent and recent media articles. You can sneak in the back door of Silicon Investor through the **Carlson Online** site. Just type in a stock symbol in the "research a company" space at the top of the home page. Among the resources Carlson will give you will be a link to Silicon Investor message board on the company you are researching. Participants on **Quicken.com**'s message boards loved the stock. Well over 80 per cent of them rated the stock a buy or strong buy. Another board to check is on the **Yahoo!Finance** site.

A CAUTIONARY NOTE ABOUT MESSAGE BOARDS

Don't believe everything you read on an Internet investing message board. On the contrary, be skeptical of everything. Message boards are full of unscrupulous investors trying to promote good-for-nothing stocks so they can drive the price up and then bail out. If you're left holding the stock, you lose. Message boards are a great place to exchange ideas, gossip and questions with other investors, so by all means use them. Just be careful out there.

www.ragingbull.com
www.siliconinvestor.com
www.carlsononline.com
www.quicken.com
finance.yahoo.com

7. What's the financial picture like at Nortel?

A good place to start is Nortel's own Web site, where the investor relations section lists all major financial news releases. How can you find a company's Web site quickly? Once again, the answer is **Carlson Online**'s company research feature. Carlson's Plus service (you have to pay for it) itself has extensive financial information, including income statements, balance sheets, retained earnings and changes in financial positions plus ratios. **Globeinvestor** offered a summary of Nortel's annual financials going back three years. The **Wright Investors' Service** report on Nortel included a historical earnings and dividends per share analysis, as well as a few ratios.

To check up on the what investors in the know are saying about Nortel's next set of quarterly numbers, the **WhisperNumber** site is the place to go. The Canadian Web site, **Q1234.com**, offers live and archived audio of corporate conference calls on quarterly earnings and other important announcements, but Nortel wasn't listed in the index. However, several other prominent companies were, including Royal Bank, Petro-Canada and Shaw Communications.

> www.carlsononline.com
> www.globeinvestor.com
> www.wisi.com
> www.whispernumber.com
> www.q1234.com

8. What have Nortel shares done lately?

The **BigCharts** site does it all-detailed quotes and zillions of different graphing possibilities that include several technical indicators. For Canadian stocks type "ca:" in front of the symbol, as in "ca:CTR.A" (Canadian Tire). A pretty good alternative for both Canadian and US stocks is **Globeinvestor**. A useful function on this site lets you compare up to three different securities or indexes on a single graph. Another Canadian alternative is **imoney**.

> www.bigcharts.com
> www.globeinvestor.com
> www.imoney.com

9. What's the insider trading and short-selling news on Nortel?

Carlson Online Plus service offers both.

Supersites: One-Stop Stock Research for Discount Broker Clients

The investing Web sites listed here will provide pretty much all the research you'll need on US stocks and, to a less extent, Canadian stocks as well. In some cases, some of these sites have built up their own library of data, but generally they group content from other sites together or provide a comprehensive set of links to other investing sites. Whichever approach they use, these supersites are an incredible resource for discount broker clients.

finance.yahoo.com: Yahoo!Finance taps into Zacks reports on both Canadian and US companies, including broker recommendations plus reams of other investing resources. To look up Canadian stocks, type the symbol and then .TO, as in CRW.TO (Cinram International Inc.).

www.411stocks.com: Type in the symbol of a US or inter-listed Canadian stock and get a concise summary of all pertinent data. Some info supplied by other sites such as the ubiquitous Zacks and **earningswhispers.com**.

www.investorhome.com: Groups together on one page the resources available at BigCharts, Justquotes, Yahoo and many others.

www.justquotes.com: If you want one-stop shopping for research on a US or inter-listed Canadian stock, this is it. Type in a stock symbol and you'll be presented with dozens of links to all the top investing sites for research, fundamentals, financials and analyst opinions.

moneycentral.msn.com: Microsoft's MoneyCentral site offers financials, charts, regulatory filings, recent news and analyst recommendations for US and Canadian stocks. For Canadians issues, type ca: and then the stock symbol, as in ca:td (Toronto-Dominion Bank.

www.quicken.com: A full package of research materials for US stocks can be found in this site's investing section. Note the alert feature, which will put up a separate window in your browser if a stock you're following makes a move, announces news or is upgraded/downgraded by analysts.

www.quote.com: Great daily coverage of US market action plus good company research for US and inter-listed Canadian companies.

www.stockfever.com/www.equityweb.com: The EquityWeb site is based on a similar concept to justquotes.com. You type in a stock symbol and it churns out the links pertaining to that company on dozens of investing Web sites, including all the biggies. Some of the links don't work, but you're very likely to find yourself overloaded with information.

www.wsrn.com: The Wall Street Research Net works along the same lines as EquityWeb, but it is a little more versatile.

How to Screen Stocks on the Web

Screening tools, sometimes called filters, are a great way to find stocks riding a wave of momentum, beat up stocks ripe for a recovery or high-yielding safety stocks. A good screening tool will let you screen all the major stock exchanges for stocks that meet a wide range of criteria set by you. For the momentum stocks, you might set your screen to pick up all shares that have gained 25 per cent or more in the past month. If you wanted a stock that still had room to run, you might arrange things so only momentum stocks with price to earnings (P/E) ratios of less than 10 or 20 were selected. This is actually pretty simple stuff as far as stock screens go. Most give you around 20 or so different parameters and one in particular—Market Guide—has 75, including 17 different financial ratios.

For Canadian Markets

Your two main choices are **Globeinvestor**, which is free, and **Carlson Online**, which costs $10 per month for a "plus-level" service package that includes a stock screen, as well as such other things as data on insider trades and short positions. Globeinvestor's is the better of the two, even though it's laid out a little awkwardly. What gives Globeinvestor the edge is the fact that it's one of a very few screening tools with a database that includes all major North American markets. Carlson only does Canada, while the majority of US screening sites focus only on stocks listed on the New York Stock Exchange, the Nasdaq stock market and the American Stock Exchange.

To use Globeinvestor's screening tool, click on the filters button on the home page. You'll find three screening categories—historical prices, intraday prices (where you'll find P/E) and company financials. Most screens have all the search criteria on one page, which is a better way to go. But Globeinvestor can still be used to effectively mine for stocks according to such factors as three-year revenue and net-income growth, market cap and price-to-book-value ratio, as well as price movements during a single day or periods ranging from one month to five years.

Once you've got a list of stocks up on your screen you can look at it in two ways: a price report, with details on recent price movement, or a financial report that looks at things like P/E and share earnings. If you're interested in P/E, just click on that column heading and the list will be reordered from highest to lowest P/E. Click again and the order is reversed.

Carlson's equity search has nine search criteria, including industry sector, share earnings, P/E ratio and performance, which is defined as trading near a 52-week high or low. For each, you can set a range, say all the TSE stocks with a P/E ratio greater than 10 and less than 20. Carlson's screening tool is well laid out, but it's not really in the league of some of the free screening tools offered on US Web sites. On the other hand, Carlson does cover all major Canadian markets.

If you're primarily interested in Canadian and US small-cap stocks, then the research tools on the **Smallcapcenter.com** Web site will likely impress you. You can search for companies using screens based on technical factors like moving averages, stochastics and so on, as well as on such things as analyst recommendations, volume and financial data such as P/E and market cap. One of the best features here is a tool that lets you type in a stock and find out which institutional investors own it.

Since there are so few screening tools dedicated to Canadian markets, it's worth pointing out the existence of a service called **ChartSmart 2000** that provides powerful filtering capabilities as well as charts and news. You download the ChartSmart software, then subscribe to either a daily or weekly data update service. Free demonstration software is available for download.

> www.globeinvestor.com
> www.carlsononline.com
> www.smallcapcenter.com
> www.chartsmart.com

For US Markets

Here you've got some real choice. There are highly technical screens for people primarily interested in financial ratios and balance sheets, all-purpose screens that cover most issues relevant to small investors and even prepackaged screens that group several search criteria together in such a way as to produce a list of undervalued stocks or fast-rising momentum stocks. The prepackaged category works well in the right hands and there are none better than those at **Microsoft MoneyCentral**.

This free site gives you plain English choices broken down into basic and advanced categories. There are six basic screens, including the highest yielding shares on the S&P 500 and large-, medium- and small-capitalization stocks with high momentum, which is defined as the largest three-month price gains compared with the rest of the market. If it was undervalued stocks you were after, you might have MoneyCentral find the cheapest stocks of large, growing companies.

MoneyCentral's 11 advanced searches require the download of a small software program, which takes less than five minutes. Once you've got the software, you can use screens with catchy names like "righteous rockets," which are defined as stocks that are profitable, have strong balance sheets and have begun to show major price appreciation, and distress stock plays, which will root out companies with a market cap of more than $50-million, a share price near its 52-week low, year-over-year revenue growth, and which are projected by analysts to post earnings growth of more than 20 per cent in the next year. MoneyCentral also gives you the option of setting your own search criteria.

Quicken.com is another Web site that takes the basic approach to screening in a very effective way. Choose from popular searches that focus on various categories of growth and value stocks or a full search with 33 variables. You can go step by step through the full search with explanations about what all the variables mean.

Another Web site that gives you the choice of predetermined screens or using your own choices is the popular **Zacks**. Among the interesting criteria used in the Zacks pre-set screen are top insider buying/selling and best best/worst change in broker recommendations over the previous week. The Zacks custom screener is unique in that it includes categories like earnings surprises and broker ratings.

Stockpoint, a good general purpose investing site, has one of the more varied menus of screening tools out there for US stocks. One will give you the top 25 stocks in all major industrial sectors ranked according to their returns over a period selected by you. You can then move up to two other screens, Stockfinder and Stockfinder Pro, the latter offering 26 different data fields.

An investing Web site called **Market Guide** offers the monster screen with 75 variables mentioned at the beginning of this section. You'll have to download free software for this screen and it takes up a substantial 15 megabytes of hard drive space. Market Guide offers a compact version of its screening tool with 20 variables, but it's not easy to use.

Another good screening tool can be found on **Hoover's Online** site. This one includes beta, a measure of a stock's volatility, among its search criteria. The **YahooFinance** stock screener includes analyst recommendations as part of its limited number of search criteria. Another site worth checking out is called **FinancialWeb**.

---

moneycentral.msn.com
www.quicken.com
www.zacks.com
www.stockpoint.com
www.marketguide.com
www.hoovers.com
screen.yahoo.com/stocks.html
www.financialweb.com/rapidresearch

How to Research a Mutual Fund on the Web

The two kingpin Web sites for researching mutual funds are Globefund and The Fund Library, but Morningstar Inc.'s move into Canada in late 1999 has introduced some formidable competition. Most discount brokers offer their own fund research tools, but generally speaking you'll find **Globefund** and **The Fund Library** offer a superior combination of a deep database and ease of use.

Now, let's say you were looking for a core Canadian equity fund. Here's how you could use the Web to sift through the hundreds of choices.

First, Separate the Good from the Bad and the Ugly

Both Globefund and The Fund Library allow you to screen funds according to several different criteria. Let's say you wanted a Canadian equity fund with a very good long-term track record of solid returns. Using either site, you could call up a list of funds that averaged 10-per-cent growth annually for the past 15 years.

More advanced searches are possible as well. For example, you could narrow the above search down by stipulating that the funds must be no load and have an MER below 2 per cent. Running this search on The Fund Library produced five different funds: Bissett Canadian Equity; OTGIF Diversified; Phillips, Hager & North Canadian Equity, Canadian Equity Plus; and Tradex Equity.

Then Narrow the List Down Further

Once you've got a list that meets your standards, you can begin to study each one closely. If you're using Globefund or The Fund Library, just click on the fund name for a link to a detailed profile. The Fund Library's profile on the Bissett fund tells you:

- The fund's inception date was March 1983
- It's RRSP-eligible
- Assets are $560-million

- MER is (a very low) 1.18 per cent
- The managers are Michael A. Quinn and Fred E. Pynn
- The top 10 holdings were BCE, Onex, Nortel, Royal Bank, Alberta Energy, Bank of Montreal, Bank of Nova Scotia, Metro-Richelieu and Power Financial.
- The fund is recommended by fund-raters Gordon Pape, Stephen Gadsden and Jonathan Chevreau.

The profile also tells you the fund's objective and strategy, gives you compound annual returns and supplies simple year-by-year returns as well.

Want to do some cross-referencing? One way is to see what fund analysis firm like Morningstar Canada has to say. Bissett and Tradex get four stars while the two PH&N funds get three on Morningstar's site.

Over at **Investcom.com**, they've set up a fund research tool that lets you pick a fund and then supplies links to resources on other sites such as Globefund's charts and The Fund Library's daily price information. As well, there's a link to Canada NewsWire to see if the company offering the fund has issued any news releases lately.

Looking for Fresh Ideas?

Morningstar Canada lets you look at the funds that have generated the most requests for profiles on the Web site, or head to the **Fund Counsel** Web site and see what the analysts there are writing about.

---

www.globefund.com
www.fundlibrary.com
www.morningstar.ca
www.investcom.com
www.fundcounsel.com

For Those Times When You Just Feel Like Surfing

These sites are the kind that you visit now and then for interesting articles, columns and stock-picking ideas, as well as to just plain further your investing education.

www.clubwallstreet.com: This site looks at daily market action and includes a menu of investor tools that will take you to other investing resources such as Wall Street City's columnists and the Hoover Online stock screener.

www.cyberinvest.com: Here is a guide to hundreds of investing sites in categories such as global investing, on-line trading, company research and investing magazines. Daily highlights are described in detail on the home page.

www.fool.com: The Motley Fool site is one of the more popular ones in the investing Web world. It offers a little of everything: suggested investing strategies, analysis and commentary, investing basics, personal finance, message boards … we could go on and on.

www.4finance.com: This is the finance version of the 4anything guide to Web sites on various subjects. A few choices are listed under headings like quotes, options, retirement planning and so forth.

www.kiplinger.com: The investing magazine's Web site includes a stock screening tool, as well as a big menu of articles on general investing themes.

www.investorama.com: Zillions of Web sites are grouped under broad headings such as on-line investing, mutual funds and "investing for life." It is kind of chaotic but fun to wallow around in.

www.ndir.com: This Canadian site has been mentioned a few times in this book because of its resources for comparing discount brokers, but it also has a quirky mix of general investing features like book picks, investing strategies, DRIPs, options and investing games.

www.nt.net/media4/business.htm: The Media4 Investment Resource Centre will keep you busy for days, guaranteed. Hundreds of sites are listed under headings like today's markets, newsletters, earnings, tool kit stuff and message boards. It lists primarily US sites but a surprising number of Canadian ones as well.

www.100hot.com/directory/business/finance.html: The 100hot site lists the week's 100 most visited financial Web sites. A mix of broker, mutual fund company, general investing and media sites.

www.onlineinvestor.com: The Web site of a magazine that is recommended reading for investors who make heavy use of on-line resources. It includes the magazine's listings on the best Web sites in various categories.

www.stockpickcentral.com: This library of investing links includes a top 100 list and a site of the week. A particularly large number of technical analysis sites are listed.

www.streetinsider.com: It links to other investing sites and includes quirky stuff like stock rumours.

www.wallstreetcity.com: This site contains market news, quotes, research tools and articles, including a "stock of the hour" feature.

www.zdii.com: The Inter@ctive Investor site is offered by publisher Ziff-Davis. It is packed with features like market updates, a research centre, message boards and more.

For Keeping an Eye on Tech Stocks

There are a number of Web sites that are helpful in researching tech stocks. Six of the best are listed.

www.cnet.com: This home page offers an index of pages on tech news, hardware reviews, consumer electronics, as well as financial and investing. You can keep track of analyst upgrades/downgrades and get broker research highlights as well. For tech stock news, go to **www.news.com**.

www.internet.com: This site describes itself as "where Wall Street meets the Web." You'll find all the latest buzz on tech IPOs, here, plus be able to keep up with Nasdaq trading with updates provided through a link to cnbc.com.

www.internetstocks.com: This sites, which bills itself as "the clear voice of reason," includes columns and news on hot tech companies, plus a "valuation calculator" that helps you "derive an estimate of your company's current market value relative to similarly modeled public companies."

www.redherring.com: This Web site by the people who put out the magazine *Red Herring*, contains tech industry news as well as market news.

www.stockjungle.com: This Web community site allows users to offer their tech stock picks. Check out the "hot picks" list, or pick a screen name for yourself and submit a stock.

www.techstockinvestor.com: This is a good site for researching tech stocks. There's also a list of 50 recommended stocks that you can look at if you pay a US$39 fee.

Technical Analysis

Technical Analysis is the science of buying and selling stocks according to their trading patterns.

www.bigcharts.com: This free stock-charting site includes several different technical indicators among its graphing parameters.

www.investortech.com: The Investor Technologies Web site includes daily US market action as seen through the prism of technical analysis.

www.sixer.com: More daily market tech analysis.

www.technimentals.com: A research site that is based on the philosophy that prudent investing analysis is based on technical as well as fundamental analysis. Some services are free, while others are reserved for paying members. Free trial memberships.

www.tradehard.com: This site bills itself as the ultimate super-site for traders and it contains vast resources on indicators, strategies and tactics. Most material is reserved for paid sub-scribers, but there's some free content as well.

Miscellaneous

www.ipomonitor.com: A good site for keeping up with hot US initial public offerings.

www.stocktrigger.com: Sign up for this free service and you'll receive a flash by e-mail, cell phone, pager or personal organizer if a stock makes a price move selected by you.

Stock Market Games

On-line stock-trading games are offered on lots of investing Web sites periodically through the year. Usually, they're done to promote the services of a particular broker or Web site. E*Trade Canada, ever eager to get its name out there in front of investors, has been a consistent game sponsor. A recent E*Trade game is called Tradersplay (**www.tradersplay.com**). It gives players $500,000 in play money to invest in pursuit of a $5,000 prize.

One of the best reasons to play these games is to learn about buying stock on your own with no risk of losing money. In fact, the best of these games are like a tutorial for on-line trading where you can familiarize yourself with the technology and the ways of the market without dropping a penny of real money. If you want to get a feel for what it's like to buy stocks on-line, then try an E*Trade game. The on-line trading screens look almost identical to E*Trade's actual ones and work pretty much the same as well. Adding to the realism is the fact that commissions are factored in and orders are executed at real-time market prices.

Another good on-line trading game offered recently was the Bay-Street.com Investment Challenge (**www.bay-street.com**). If you can't find the game on this site, try **www.investor factory.com**, which offers a game on which the Bay-Street.com one is based. Where these two games excel is in their realism. Both allow you to place a market order or a limit order, whereas most games just allow you to use a market order. (The differences between these was discussed in Chapter 6.) If you want to see the differing results you can get from using both types of orders, this game is a great place to do it without incurring any real money losses.

For example, you could pick a hot technology stock and put in a market order after the stock market closed for the day. Next, you'd watch the following morning to see the price at which your order was executed. The execution price may well be a lot higher than the previous day's closing price. That's a potentially expensive lesson to learn with real money.

Another recently available game worth checking out is the investment challenge offered on the TSE Web site at **www.tse.com**. The attraction here is that you can trade options and mutual funds as well as stocks and employ more sophisticated techniques such as buying on margin and short selling. Adding to the realism in this game is the fact that you can do limit and stop-loss orders as well as market orders. Trading commissions, dividends and stock splits are factored in as well.

---

www.tradesplay.com

www.bay-street.com

www.investorfactory.com

www.tse.com

Check out even a fraction of the Web sites listed here and you'll likely feel a whopping case of information overload coming on. One solution is to pick a favourite half dozen or so sites and bookmark them for regular use. For instance, you might want to pick an all-purpose financial site for news and stock market commentary, a research site for looking up stocks, a high-tech site and a favourite message board. Don't forget to check other sites from time to time, though. In order to survive, financial Web sites must constantly improve by adding new material and features. Some sites don't make it, which explains why there may be some Web addresses in this chapter that no longer work.

Conclusion:
The Future of Discounters

The discount brokerage industry has progressed amazingly since its Canadian inception 15 years ago and will evolve even faster over the next few years. As we were writing and researching this book, numerous changes took place in the industry. For instance, the US giant Charles Schwab Corp. entered the Canadian market and insurer Sun Life Assurance began to promote a discount service of its own. As well, discounters en masse cut their mutual fund commission rates and vastly expanded the amount of research they offered clients. Another big change was that Toronto-Dominion Bank dropped the well known Green Line name for its Canadian discount operation and renamed it TD Waterhouse.

In the coming months and years, we will see technology further enable average investors to manage their accounts and we'll see more and more research become available to discount clients. On the technological front, look for wireless trading to become widely available. Several brokers, including TD Waterhouse and Scotia Discount Brokerage, went into 2000 with plans to introduce a service that allows clients to check their accounts, get quotes and make trades from PCS telephones equipped with Web browsers from linking to the Internet.

Here are some other changes to look out for in the discount brokerage industry:

- A key development happened just as this book went to press. After much lobbying by discounters, securities regulators have allowed discounters to enter trades without doing a suitability check.

- The impact of this change is significant. For one thing, some room was created for commissions to fall because of the time saved with representatives no longer having to do suitability checks on each trade. As well, it was expected that response times on the phone and particularly on-line would improve, as would trade execution speeds. With the demise of the suitability check, it was also expected that the account application process would become more stringent. Brokers will be more careful about accepting accounts from clients without investing knowledge, and each discounter will have clients sign forms saying they are aware that their broker provides nothing in the way of advice or recommendations.

- The differences between discounters and full-serve brokers will blur. Bank of Nova Scotia, Canadian Imperial Bank of Commerce, Bank of Montreal, Royal Bank and Toronto-Dominion Bank (to a lesser degree) will merge the services of their financial management divisions for full-serve and discount brokers. The separate brands will endure, but clients will be encouraged to trade both solo through a discounter and through an adviser as well.

- Discounters will make greater efforts to cultivate the conservative long-term investor as well as the aggressive trader.

- More firms will allow clients to trade on international markets.

- More Canadians will open accounts with US discounters to take advantage of the lower commissions, more extensive research and lower MER mutual funds.

- New players will challenge the dozen discounters covered in this book, possibly US deep discounters such as Datek Online or Ameritrade. Among the new domestic competitors is eNorthern, an electronic brokerage and Internet marketing venture that was built through the acquisition and merger of two smaller, established Canadian brokerage firms.

- There will be more aggressive marketing of RESP investing. Discounters that don't offer RESPs soon will. It's a virtually untapped market for the brokers and offers a opportunity for long-term relationship building.

- Bond trading on-line will proliferate. When a stock market correction happens, many investors will flee to the comparitive security of the fixed-income market, and on-line bond trading will become a necessity.

Changes made by regulators and stock markets around the world will also affect discount brokers, as will changes in investor behaviour. Here are a few likely possibilities:

- The New York and other exchanges will start to quote all stock listings in decimals rather than fractions.

- Exchanges will extend trading hours.

- Stock trades will be settled in a day instead of the current three days.

- Companies will make more use of the Internet to keep shareholders updated on their activities. Some firms are already releasing their earnings and making news announcements on-line.

- The globalization of markets will mean that companies will list on multiple exchanges wherever their products are offered.

- Index mutual funds will proliferate, while interest in actively managed mutual funds will taper off somewhat.

- New types of index participation units will be introduced and investors will respond by buying more of these overlooked mutal fund alternatives. Index participation units trade like a stock but offer performance that mirrors a particular stock index.

- Some companies will carry out their initial public offerings on-line, allowing them to avoid the high costs of using full-service brokers as underwriters.

You've probably noticed a common theme to the changes we've outlined here. Virtually all of them are likely to make investing with a discount broker more appealing. Even the service delays that have so angered investors will improve thanks to the easing of the KYC rule for discounters. Still, discount brokers still aren't for everybody. As we saw in Chapter One, you need time and investing knowledge, or at least the willingness to learn, in order to use a discounter effectively. But the fact remains that in the years ahead, having a discount broker account will be nearly as common as owning a mutual fund is now. The point of this book is to help make do-it-yourself investing all it can be for these new discount clients. Happy trading.

Index